Favourite Recipes
Books for Cooks
number four, five and six

By

Eric Treuillé
Victoria Blashford-Snell
Jennifer Joyce
Olivia Greco
Ursula Ferrigno
Celia Brooks Brown

Decorated by Selina Snow

PRYOR PUBLICATIONS
WHITSTABLE AND WALSALL
Specialist in Facsimile Reproductions
MEMBER OF
INDEPENDENT PUBLISHERS GUILD

75 Dargate Road, Yorkletts, Whitstable,
Kent CT5 3AE, England
Tel. & Fax (01227) 274655
E-mail: alan@pryor-publications.co.uk
www.pryor-publications.co.uk
Kent Exporter of the Year Awards
Shortlisted
International Business Awards
A full list of publications sent free on request.

© BOOKS FOR COOKS October 2005
ISBN 1-905253-06-0
Cover by Selina Snow
Compiled by Rosie Kindersley
Published by Pryor Publications
For
BOOKS FOR COOKS
Tel: 0207 221 1992
Fax: 0207 221 1517
E-mail: info@booksforcooks.com
Website: www.booksforcooks.com

Printed and bound by
Estudios Graficos ZURE, S.A.
48950 – Erandio (Spain)

CONTENTS

SO MUCH HAS HAPPENED this year at Books for Cooks that we're not quite sure where to begin. Of course the big news of the year is that Eric and Rosie are now the proud owners of Books for Cooks. It is nearly ten years now since Rosie walked into Books for Cooks and Heidi, with her inimitable mix of insight and inspiration, offered her a job on the spot. Then Eric walked into Books for Cooks and into Rosie's life (a story that Heidi loves to tell, still making Rosie blush as deeply today as on the very day itself in June 1993). When Heidi left to live in Tuscany (where she now devotes her considerable energy to cookery holidays - see **www.theitaliancookingschool.com** for details) and the question of what next arose, Rosie and Eric just couldn't imagine life without Books for Cooks.

As proud as we all are of Books for Cooks, this was the year we finally admitted that our beloved shop was in need of a face-lift. Our book shelves were bowing and bending, our test kitchen counter was warping and that silly green phone just wouldn't stay on the wall - indeed our long-distance customers may recall the great crash as it fell to the ground, again! So a decision was made - Books for Cooks would be refurbished.

Much soul-searching took place before we embarked upon this massive upheaval. Books for Cooks had been a second home for many of us and it was difficult to imagine any changes at all. Then there were long discussions with anxious customers as they begged us not to change the shop's special atmosphere. And, as we began to spread the word of impending disruption more widely, there were the gasps of disbelief. In fact, certain customers took to coming for lunch or popping in for a browse and a coffee several times a week to stock up on their Books for Cooks fix before several months of deprivation.

We are pretty confident, however, that, on your next visit to 4 Blenheim Crescent, your gasps will be of delight. The essentials remain the same - shelves crammed with cookbooks still line the walls from floor to ceiling and sweet scents of baking cakes mingled with the more savoury aromas of frying garlic and onion still fill the air. The most significant (and, we feel, exciting) change is the removal of the wall at the back of the shop that divided the tables and chairs from the test kitchen and the rest of the book shop. Another exciting change is a fabulously foodie mural painted by our in-house artist (and illustrator of these little books) Selina Snow. And don't panic, there's still a squashy Books for Cooks sofa for book browsing. Its location may have changed, but Books for Cooks wouldn't be Books for Cooks without a comfy sofa!

While downstairs was crawling with builders - and plumbers, and electricians, and carpenters, and decorators - we were all tucked away on the second floor of 4 Blenheim Crescent, hard at work on our fifth little recipe book. Writing it felt rather like an act of good faith - faith that the cooks and books would soon be back in their right and proper place at Books for Cooks.

But it's certainly not all change at Books for Cooks. The daily ritual of a testing and tasting lunch (on which this series of little cookbooks is based) still goes on, when we all sit down to eat and discuss the day's tested recipes. Our cookery workshops, founded by Eric and Ursula in 1995, take place nearly every day now, so there is cooking up and down stairs at Books for Cooks. This little book is the fruit of that entire culinary endeavour.

THE BOOKS FOR COOKS COOKS

ERIC TREUILLÉ was born in Cahors in South West France. At the age of thirteen he was apprenticed as a *charcutier*; he went on to complete his culinary studies in Paris. Work as a restaurant chef took him from Paris to London, where he began a new career working as a food stylist with Anne Willan and Le Cordon Bleu cooking school. He discovered Books for Cooks, his wife Rosie Kindersley and a whole new career as combined cookery teacher, food writer and bookseller all on one fateful day in June 1993 when he crossed the threshold of 4 Blenheim Crescent.

VICTORIA BLASHFORD SNELL has been cooking full time since she was sixteen. She trained at Le Cordon Bleu cooking school, but credits her culinary creativity to her travels with her father and her husband, who are both explorers, and to her involvement with Books for Cooks where she has been cooking since 1992. She runs a highly successful catering company that combines her talents of cooking and organisation with her love of drama and occasion - but still finds time to teach workshops at Books for Cooks.

JENNIFER JOYCE is a self-taught cook from the States. Her love of food began early while cooking for her Italian family of eleven! Until the birth of her first son Liam (since followed by a second, Riley) Jennifer was one of the mainstays of the Test Kitchen. She now concentrates on food writing and teaching. Her workshops focus on New American cooking - especially Southwestern, Fusion and Californian - and unusual ingredients and big bold flavours are very much the trademark of her classes.

URSULA FERRIGNO grew up on her father's vegetable and olive producing farm in southern Italy where she was taught to cook by her grandmother. She discovered Books for Cooks in 1991, when we were recommended as an ideal location for her popular Italian Day cookery demonstrations. She is the busiest person we know! In between writing a steady stream of wonderful cookbooks, she finds time to teach workshops at Books for Cooks and give cookery classes at cooking schools both in Italy and up and down the British Isles.

Italian-born OLIVIA GRECO lived for many years in Mexico and the USA before returning to her roots in Tuscany. Cooking was always at the heart of family life as her mother was a passionate cook and Olivia her willing assistant, so cooking professionately was a natural career choice. In 1999 she met Heidi Lascelles who persuaded her to leave her long - standing post as a chef in a Tuscan *fattoria* and devote herself to a teaching cookery, both for Books for Cooks in London.

American- born CELIA BROOKS BROWN says that the very first day she walked into Books for Cooks she realised she'd arrived in a cook's pardise. She asked for a job at once! She began selling books in the shop but couldn't keep out of the kitchen for long, where her inspired and eclectic style of vegetarian cookery soon made its mark.

After a variety of careers working (and eating) around the globe, American-born PAM SHOOKMAN took the plunge and did what she'd always wanted to do: become a cook. After training at Leith's she began life as a chef with Bill Sewell at The Place Below, before becoming Ursula Ferrigno's assistant at RJS restaurant and bakery. Sure of a good match, Ursula introduced Pam to the rest of the Books for Cooks team at a jolly dinner at Kensington Place restaurant. Pam says she is forever grateful - and we don't mind admitting that we are too!

Boston-born SARAH BENJAMIN started out professional life as a biochemist - actually an extremely useful training for a cook. However, her love of food and cooking - she spent all her spare time reading cookery magazines and overwhelming family and friends with culinary delights - soon took over and she left her research post to work at Hamersley's Bistro (renowned as Julia Child's favourite Boston restaurant) where she rapidly progressed from dog's body to pastry chef. Love and marriage bought her to these shores and Books for Cooks was, she says, quite naturally her first port of call on arriving in London.

COOK BOOKS BY THE BOOKS FOR COOKS COOKS...

Favourite Recipes From Books for Cooks 1, 2 & 3 Victoria Blashford Snell, Jennifer Joyce, Eric Treuillé, Ursula Ferrigno, Sophie Braimbridge & Celia Brooks Brown (2001 Pryor Publications)

Diva Cooking Victoria Blashford Snell & Jennifer Joyce (2001 Mitchell Beazley)

Canapés Eric Treuillé & Victoria Blashford Snell (1999 Dorling Kindersley)

Cordon Bleu Complete Cooking Techniques Eric Treuillé (1996 Cassell)

Bread Eric Treuillé & Ursula Ferrigno (1999 Dorling Kindersley)

Barbecue Eric Treuillé and Birgit Erath (2000 Dorling Kindersley)

Pasta Eric Treuillé & Anna Del Conte (2000 Dorling Kindersley)

The Well-Dressed Salad Jennifer Joyce (2004 Pavilion Books)

Truly Italian Ursula Ferrigno (1999 Mitchell Beazley)

Risotto Ursula Ferrigno (2001 Ryland, Peters and Small)

Bringing Italy Home Ursula Ferrigno (2001 Mitchell Beazley)

Italian Cakes & Pastries Ursula Ferrigno (1997 Metro Books)

Real Fast Vegetarian Food Ursula Ferrigno (2002 Metro Books)

Truly Madly Pasta Ursula Ferrigno (2003 Quadrille Publications)

Italy Sea to Sky Ursula Ferrigno (2003 Mitchell Beazley)

Trattoria Ursula Ferrigno (2004 Mitchell Beazley)

Vegetarian Foodscape Celia Brooks Brown (1998 Pen and Ink)

New Vegetarian Celia Brooks Brown (2001 Ryland, Peters and Small)

New Kitchen Garden Celia Brooks Brown with Adam Caplan (2003 Ryland, Peters and Small)

Entertaining Vegetarians Celia Brooks Brown (2003 Pavilion Books)

Low-Carb Vegetarian Celia Brooks Brown (2004 Pavilion Books)

... AND SOME OF THEIR FAVOURITE COOKBOOKS

Avoca Café Cookbook Hugo Arnold with Leylie Hayes (2000 Avoca Handweavers)
How to be a Domestic Goddess Nigella Lawson (2000 Chatto & Windus)
Living & Eating Annie Bell with John Pawson (2001 Ebury Press)
Moro The Cookbook Sam & Sam Clark (2001 Ebury Press)
More Simple Café Food Julie le Clerc (2000 Penguin)
Seductive Flavours of the Levant -Traditional Home Cooking from Lebanon, Syria and Turkey Nada Saleh (2002 Robson Books)
Simple Café Food Julie Le Clerc (1999 Penguin)
Simple Food Jill Dupleix (2002 Quadrille Publications)
Soup Simply Sensational Mathew Drennan (2000 Aquamarine)
Sydney Food Bill Granger (2000 Murdoch)

PLEASE NOTE! For any out of print cookbooks, we thoroughly recommend that you contact -

Liz Seeber on 01273 684 949

Cooking The Books on 01633 400150

NOTES ON THE RECIPES

BEFORE YOU COOK read through the recipe carefully. Make sure you have all the equipment and ingredients required.

ACCURATE MEASUREMENTS are essential if you want consistently good results each time. Always stick to one set of measurements, whether, imperial, metric or American cups, and never mix and match.

PREHEAT YOUR OVEN for 10-20 minutes before you need to use it. Bear in mind that the higher the temperature required, the longer it will take to preheat the oven.

OVENS DO VARY from kitchen to kitchen - so it's most worthwhile getting to know your own! Most have hot spots, so be prepared to rotate dishes from top to bottom or from front to back during cooking time. A good oven thermometer is invaluable! If using a fan assisted oven, do follow the instructions for adjusting cooking timings and temperatures.

FRUIT AND VEGETABLES should be washed, trimmed and, unless otherwise stated in the recipe's ingredients list, peeled.

ALWAYS TASTE FOOD as you cook and before you serve. Ingredients differ from day to day, season to season, kitchen to kitchen. Be prepared to adjust sweetness, sharpness, spiciness, and, most important of all, salt, to your own taste.

BUY THE BEST you can afford. Whatever your cooking skills, the end result can only be as good as the ingredients you put in. Now that the Farmers' Market movement is beginning to grow in Britain, we should all soon have the opportunity to buy food that is not only seasonal but also produced locally and on a smaller scale. Call The National Association of Farmers' Markets on 01225 787914 or see their website (**www.farmersmarkets.net**).

USE ORGANIC EGGS because, unless you know the supplier, the term free-range generally has little or no meaning. By organic we mean **Soil Association Certified**, because all other standards (including, at the time of writing, even the RSPCA Freedom Foods label) allow the unacceptably cruel practice of de-beaking.

LET US KNOW if you can't get a recipe to work. Please call us (even if you are in the middle of cooking a recipe!) so that we can help. Despite triple testing, mistakes do creep in, usually at the computer stage, we're afraid. Corrections can then be included in the next print run. Thank you!

Soups

TOMATO, LENTIL AND ORANGE SOUP

An inspired ingredient combination that makes a prettily orange-looking, deliciously orange-tasting and gorgeously orange-scented soup. We owe it to the excellent *Avoca Café Cookbook*, written by the always reliable Hugo Arnold with Leylie Hayes.

SERVES 4

2 organic oranges (wash and scrub well if not organic)
60 g (2 oz/½ stick) butter
1 onion, chopped
4 garlic cloves, crushed
¼ tsp crushed chilli flakes
400 g (14 oz) tin of Italian plum tomatoes, chopped
60 g (2 oz/⅓ cup) red lentils
300 ml (½ pint/2 ¼ cups) hot stock or water
salt, black pepper
2 tsp finely chopped fresh mint or parsley to sprinkle

GRATE THE ZEST from the oranges. Cut the peel from the oranges (with a sharp or serrated knife, cut a slice from each end, then cut away the peel, following the curve of the fruit and removing as much of the white pith and skin as possible). Cut the peeled oranges into chunks over a bowl, saving as much of the juices as possible.

Melt the butter in a large pot over medium heat. Add the onion and cook, stirring, until softened, about 5 minutes. Add the garlic, orange zest and chilli and cook until the onions smell garlicky and citrusy, about 1 minute. Then tip in the orange pieces and juices, tomatoes and lentils, give it all a good stir, and pour in the hot stock or water. Bring to the boil and simmer steadily, with the lid on, stirring every now and then, until the lentils are soft, about 25 minutes. The soup will appetisingly perfume your kitchen with savoury orange aromas as it cooks.

Put the soup in a food processor (you may need to do this in batches) and pulse until smooth. Return the soup to the rinsed out pan, thin with water if necessary and reheat until piping hot. Add salt and pepper to taste. Serve hot in warmed bowls. A sprinkling of finely chopped fresh herbs will nicely highlight this beautifully orange-coloured and flavoured soup.

THINK AHEAD
The soup can be made a day ahead; cool completely before covering and chilling.

SAFFRON SCENTED SEAFOOD SOUP WITH FENNEL & AIOLI

It's a real challenge to gather together the whole Books for Cooks family, but every year, we manage it somehow. This gorgeous soup reminds us of a particularly memorable Books for Cooks party on a crisp winter day in Wiltshire. The menu was based around the classic Books for Cooks repertoire: soup, savoury tarts and meringues - plus a glazed Wiltshire ham served with home made chutneys and Cumberland sauce in deference to season and locale. This soup made up the first course, and the cooks have been asking Victoria for the recipe ever since.

SERVES 4

4 scallops
8 raw peeled tiger prawns (large shrimp)
(125 g) 4 oz monkfish tail, cut into 2 ½ cm (1 inch) pieces

FOR THE BROTH
2 tbsp olive oil
2 garlic cloves, crushed
1 onion, peeled and finely chopped
½ fennel bulb, finely diced
1 small carrot, finely diced
1 glass of dry white wine
750 ml (1 ¼ pints/3 cups) hot fish or vegetable stock
2 ripe tomatoes, seeded and finely diced
1 small potato (about 60 g (2 oz)), finely diced
a large pinch of saffron threads
4 tbsp lemon juice
salt, black pepper, cayenne pepper
fresh dill sprigs to garnish

FOR THE AIOLI
2 organic egg yolks
1 tsp creamy Dijon mustard
2 garlic cloves, crushed

1 tbsp lemon juice
½ tsp salt
¼ tsp white sugar
150 ml (5 fl oz/ ⅔ cup) sunflower oil
150 ml (5 fl oz/ ⅔ cup) olive oil

WARM THE OIL in a pan over medium heat, add the garlic, onion, fennel and carrot and cook, stirring, until softened, about 5 minutes. Pour in the wine, bring to the boil and bubble furiously for a couple of minutes to allow the alcohol to evaporate. Add the stock, tomatoes, potatoes and saffron, bring back to the boil, then simmer gently until the vegetables are tender, about 15 minutes. Stir in the lemon juice and season to taste with salt, pepper and cayenne.

While the soup is simmering, make the aioli. Make sure all the ingredients are at room temperature before you begin. You need a bowl and a whisk. Place the bowl on a cloth to stop it slipping as you whisk. Whisk the egg yolk, mustard, garlic, lemon juice, salt and sugar until thick and creamy. Put both oils in a jug. Whisk in the oil a drop at a time until the mixture thickens. Add the remaining oil in a thin, steady stream, whisking constantly until thick and glossy. The whole process only takes a couple of minutes. You can of course use a blender or a food processor, but you may need to stop the machine at intervals to scrape down the sides and over the base of the bowl with a spatula, depending on the capacity of your machine. Taste to check the flavour, adding more lemon or seasoning as necessary.

To finish, adjust the heat so that the soup is barely simmering. Add the fish to the hot broth and poach very gently (the liquid should "tremble" rather than bubble) until cooked through, about 5 minutes. Ladle into warmed bowls, making sure the shellfish is evenly distributed (a slotted spoon is useful for this). Serve at once, garnished with dill sprigs and a generously heaped spoonful of aioli.

THINK AHEAD
You could make the broth either the day before (keep it covered and chilled), but the seafood must be added to the hot broth just before serving. The broth also freezes very well. The aioli can also be made a day (and up to 3 days) in advance. Keep covered and chilled but return to room temperature before stirring to avoid curdling.

CHESTNUT & CHORIZO SOUP

Our most favourite soup in the book - we remain eternally grateful to Sam and Sam Clark and their *Moro The Cookbook* for its creation. Its pairing of sweetly nutty chestnuts and lightly caramelised vegetables with the mild heat of the paprika-seasoned sausage and a hint of dried chilli is culinary perfection incarnate.

If you can't locate any chorizo sausage (available in Spanish and Portuguese shops, good delicatessens, department store food halls and the deli counter of large supermarkets), you can usually find ready sliced chorizo along with the packets of sliced hams and salamis in supermarkets.

You can use fresh chestnuts; you'll need about 500 g (1 lb). They are rather a pain to peel, as their shells come away easily enough once they are cooked but their inner skin clings tight. Score their skins and bake at 150 C (300 F) Gas 2 for 15 minutes. Allow them to cool just a little as they are definitely easier to peel while still hot from the oven (hot tip: use a tea-towel or wear washing-up gloves). Squeeze the shell to crack open, then use a small sharp knife to lever off both shell and skin.

SERVES 4

a pinch of saffron threads
4 tbsp olive oil
1 large onion, finely chopped
1 medium carrot, diced
1 celery stick, diced
200 g (7 oz) chorizo sausage, skinned and diced
3 garlic cloves, crushed
1 tsp ground cumin
1 ½ tsp finely chopped fresh thyme leaves
¼ tsp dried chilli flakes
2 tomatoes, fresh, large and ripe or tinned Italian plum,
      roughly chopped
400 g (14 oz) cooked peeled chestnuts
      (we use vacuum packed for sheer ease), roughly chopped
1 litre (1 ¾ pints/4 cups) hot stock or water
salt, black pepper

PLACE THE SAFFRON in a small bowl and pour over a few tablespoons of boiling water. Set aside while you start the soup.

Warm the oil in large pot over a medium high heat. Add the onion, carrot, celery, and chorizo and fry briskly, stirring occasionally, until the onions are golden and all the vegetables are browned and caramelised at the edges, about 15 minutes.

Stir in the garlic, cumin, thyme and chilli and cook until fragrant, another minute. Add the tomatoes and when the tomatoes are bubbling, add the chestnuts. Pour in the hot stock or water and the saffron threads and their golden liquid. Bring to the boil, adjust the heat and simmer steadily for 10 minutes. Remove from the heat and, using a hand-held blender, whiz the soup until smooth-ish but still with some texture. If you don't have a hand-held blender, use a potato masher or transfer to a food processor and use the pulse button. Thin with hot water as needed and season to taste with salt and pepper. Reheat and ladle into warmed bowls and serve at once.

RED BEAN & CHORIZO SOUP A more economical version replaces the chestnuts with two drained and well-rinsed 400 g (14 oz) tins of red kidney beans.

SWEET POTATO SOUP WITH GINGER & COCONUT

Notting Hill's Caribbean community has always ensured the steady supply of sweet potatoes on Portobello Road Market. Recently, however, we have found these dusty red tubers with their moist dense flesh more widely available. And what a good thing too - sweet spuds make a fabulous mash (see page 130 in Victoria and Jennifer's *Diva Cooking*) as well as a nice change from the more usual baked potato, especially when served with a squeeze of lime, while on page 66 in this little volume you'll find Jill Dupleix's fabulous Chorizo & Sweet Potato Salad.

This rather rich and luxurious soup pairs these sweet-fleshed spuds with the totally tropical flavours of coconut, ginger and coriander, and we found it in Julie Le Clerc's superlative *More Simple Café Food*. If you find that you are defeated in your quest for sweet potatoes, we suggest using butternut squash instead.

SERVES 4

3 tbsp sunflower oil
2 onions, finely chopped
2 garlic cloves, chopped
500 g (1 lb) sweet potatoes, sliced (see ingredients note below)
1 medium potato, sliced
2 cm (¾ inch) piece of fresh ginger, grated
½ tsp salt
750ml (1 ¼ pints/3 cups) hot chicken or vegetable stock
250 ml (8 fl oz/1 cup) coconut milk (don't forget to shake
       the tin well before opening)
Tabasco
2 tbsp finely chopped fresh coriander (cilantro)
1 spring onion (scallion), sliced diagonally

WARM THE OIL in a large pot (with a lid) over a low heat. Stir in the onions, garlic, potatoes and ginger, sprinkle over the salt, add half a cupful of water, cover and leave to sweat gently for 15 minutes, stirring occasionally, until the vegetables have softened and smell sweetly gingery. Pour in the hot stock, bring to the boil and simmer gently until the vegetables are very soft, about 20 minutes. Put the soup with the coconut milk into a food processor (you may have to do this in batches) and pulse until smooth. Return the soup to the rinsed out pan and thin with hot water as needed (you're aiming for quite a rich and creamy soup), then add salt and Tabasco to taste. Reheat gently, without boiling, until piping hot. Ladle the soup into warmed bowls, scatter with the coriander and spring onion garnish and serve immediately.

INGREDIENTS NOTE
Always choose the most common sweet potato with reddy brown skin as it has bright orange flesh and a sweet creamy starchy flavour. Purple skinned sweet potatoes are white fleshed and too sugary sweet.

CAULIFLOWER & CRÈME FRAÎCHE SOUP

Yes, there is life for the somewhat despised and rather under-used *choufleur* post "cauliflower cheese", as this superbly simple soup courtesy of Annie Bell (from her *Living & Eating*) perfectly demonstrates. In fact, when truly fresh, cauliflowers are sweet and delicate rather than aggressively cabbagey.

The innovative Julie Le Clerc uses cauliflower to great effect in *More Simple Café Food* - Roast Cauliflower Salad with Caper Crumbs. Ursula's *Truly Italian* includes a number of splendid Italian ways with cauliflower, including a chilli-spiked pasta dish and a refreshingly piquant winter salad.

How to tell if it's fresh? The leaves attached to the stalk are the best indicator - they should be bright green and squeaky fresh.

SERVES 4

1 medium cauliflower (about 750 g (1 ½ lb))
60 g (2 oz/½ stick) butter
1 large onion, sliced
1 medium potato, sliced
½ tsp salt
1 litre (1 ¼ pints/4 cups) hot chicken or vegetable stock
4 tbsp crème fraîche
black pepper, freshly grated nutmeg
1 tbsp finely chopped chives to garnish

CUT THE CAULIFLOWER into quarters, then cut out the stem and core and discard. Cut the cauliflower into 2 ½ cm (1 inch) pieces. Melt the butter in a large pot (with a lid) over a low heat. Add the cauliflower, onion and potato with half a cupful of water, sprinkle over the salt, cover and let stew slowly for 15 minutes, until the vegetables are tender and buttery. Pour in the hot stock and simmer steadily for another 15 minutes, when the vegetables will be very soft. Put the soup and the crème fraîche in a food processor (you may have to do this in batches) and pulse until silky smooth. Return the soup to the rinsed out pan and thin with hot water as needed. Season to taste with salt, pepper and nutmeg. Reheat gently and serve in warmed bowls garnished with a sprinkling of chives.

CAULIFLOWER & BLUE CHEESE SOUP A rather sophisticated soup. Add 60 g (2 oz) blue cheese to the soup with the crème fraîche.

CAULIFLOWER CHEESE & MUSTARD SOUP Cold weather comfort food par excellence, courtesy of Nigel Slater and his *Real Food.* Stir 1 ½ tbsp of grainy mustard into the soup, grate 175 g (6 oz/2 cups) real Cheddar or Gruyère cheese and sprinkle each serving with cheese.

SMOKED HADDOCK CHOWDER WITH SWEETCORN & SQUASH

Stop! Don't pass this recipe! Yes, we know it sounds an unlikely ingredient combination, but this stunning soup is a real sunburst of colours and flavours - in fact Eric says it's his favourite soup of the year. We found it in Mathew Drennan's *Soup Simply Sensational* - a book that is truly a must for all soup lovers, chock-full as it is of similarly brilliant innovations.

The sweetcorn kernels are Eric's little addition which, he feels, enhances the recipe's chowder-iness, as well as throwing in an extra splash of sunny colour to set off the mellow pink and orange hues of the soup.

SERVES 4

500 g (1 lb) smoked haddock fillets
60 g (2 oz/4 tbsp) butter
1 onion, finely chopped
400 g (14 oz) butternut squash (about half a medium
    squash), cubed
2 orange-fleshed sweet potatoes, cubed
300 ml (10 fl oz/1 ¼ cups) water
600 ml (1 pint/2 ½ cups) milk
2 cobs of corn, kernels stripped with a knife or 150 g
    (5 oz/1 cup) frozen sweetcorn kernels, defrosted
4 tbsp double (heavy) cream
1 handful fresh basil, sliced

SKIN THE HADDOCK. This is very easy. Hold one end of the fish fillet - the tail end if the fillets are whole. Make a cut across the flesh but not through the skin. Insert the knife in the cut at a slight angle and move the knife between the flesh and the skin with a sawing action until you reach the other end of the fillet. Discard the skin and cut the flesh into 2 ½ by 2 ½ cm (1 by 1 inch) pieces.

Melt the butter in a large pan over medium heat, add the onion and cook until just soft, about 5 minutes. Add the squash and sweet potato and cook, stirring, until just starting to soften round the edges, 5 minutes. Add the water, bring to the boil, adjust the heat and simmer steadily until the squash and the potato are tender, 10-15 minutes.

With a potato masher, give a couple of good mashes to the soup to break up some of the squash and sweet potato cubes and give the soup a little body. Add the milk, bring just to a simmer, then add the haddock and sweet corn. Cook at a bare simmer until the haddock is cooked through and flakes easily, about 5 minutes. Stir in the cream and basil. Thin with water or milk if necessary and add salt and pepper to taste. Serve hot in warmed bowls.

THINK AHEAD
The soup can be made a day ahead up to the point when you add the haddock and corn. Cool the soup completely before covering and chilling. Reheat to a simmer, then add the haddock, corn, cream and basil as directed.

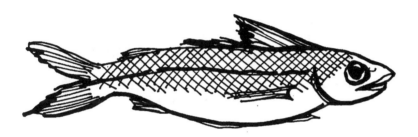

LENTIL, COCONUT
& WILTED SPINACH SOUP

Inventive east-meets-west cuisine from our very own Celia Brooks Brown and her fabulous second cookbook *New Vegetarian*. You can come and see Celia's very special brand of meatless cuisine - abounding in other such inspired flavour combinations in action at one of her cookery classes upstairs at Books for Cooks.

SERVES 4

150 g (5 oz/1 cup) puy lentils
1 litre (1 ¾ pints/4 cups) hot chicken or vegetable stock
1 onion, finely chopped
3 garlic cloves, finely chopped
2 tsp ground cumin
250 ml (8 fl oz/1 cup) tinned coconut milk (shake the tin well before
   opening)
2-3 tbsp dark soy sauce
4 small handfuls (about 50 g/2 oz) of baby spinach
salt, black pepper

PLACE THE LENTILS with water just to cover in a large pot over medium heat. Bring to the boil and simmer steadily for 10 minutes. Add the hot stock, onion, garlic, cumin, coconut milk and soy sauce. Simmer gently until the lentils are tender, 20-30 minutes. Thin the soup with water if necessary and add salt, pepper and extra soy sauce to taste.

Divide the spinach leaves among 4 warmed bowls and ladle the hot soup on top. The heat from the soup will wilt the leaves and turn them bright green. Serve at once.

THINK AHEAD
The soup can be made a day ahead, but do not add the spinach until just before serving. Cool the lentil and coconut broth completely before covering and chilling.

MINTED PEA SOUP

An old favourite from *Avoca Café Cookbook* that is also excellent when served chilled. Except for the fresh mint, most people have most of these ingredients to hand most of the time, so, if you use a teaspoonful of dried mint (or even ½ teaspoonful of mint sauce) instead of the fresh, this lovely soup becomes an entirely storecupboard standby.

If fresh peas are abundantly in season or in your garden, you'll need about 1 kg (2 lb) of peas in their pods instead of the frozen peas. Unless they're tiny and straight out of the garden (in which case we feel it might be rather a waste to use them for soup!) you'll need to cook them for about 3 minutes before whizzing.

SERVES 4

60 g (2 oz/¼ stick) butter
1 onion, chopped
1 medium potato, roughly chopped
1 litre (1 ¾ pints/4 cups) hot stock or water
350 g (12 oz) frozen petit pois
1 handful of fresh mint, finely chopped
125 ml (4 fl oz/½ cup) milk or cream
salt, black pepper

MELT THE BUTTER in a pan over a low heat. Add the onion and cook gently until softened but not coloured, about 10 minutes. Add the potato with the hot stock or water, turn the heat to medium and bring to the boil. Adjust the heat, cover and simmer steadily until the potato is cooked through, about 20 minutes. Add the peas, bring back to the boil and simmer, uncovered, until tender, 1-2 minutes.

Put the soup with the mint in a food processor and pulse until smooth. Return the soup to the rinsed out pan and stir in the milk or cream. Thin with hot water if necessary, and reheat gently until piping hot, but not boiling. Add salt and pepper to taste. Ladle the soup into warmed bowls and serve at once. Or, serve chilled. After whizzing in the food processor, let it cool completely, then stir in the cold milk or cream, adjust the consistency with cold water, season to taste, and chill.

CREAMY POTATO SOUP
WITH ROCKET PESTO

Creamy without being cloying, this deeply velvety soup was a huge hit this winter at Books for Cooks. And the secret of its success? Not cream, but cream cheese. A stroke of genius courtesy of the immensely talented Julie Le Clerc and her *Simple Café Food*. We've since used goat's (instead of cream) cheese to even greater applause.

The pesto doesn't have to be of the rocket (arugula) variety. Fresh basil, flat-leaf parsley or baby spinach would all be lovely too.

SERVES 4

15 g (½ oz/1 tbsp) butter
1 tbsp olive oil
2 onions, chopped
4 garlic cloves
1 kg (2 lb) potatoes, roughly chopped
1 litre (1 ¾ pints/4 cups hot stock or water
125 g (4 oz/ ½ cup) cream cheese or fresh, creamy goat's cheese
salt, black pepper

FOR THE PESTO
4 garlic cloves
1 handful (about 15 g/ ½ oz) of rocket (arugula)
2 tbsp pine nuts
4 tbsp grated Parmesan
3 tbsp olive oil

MELT THE BUTTER with the oil in a pan over a low heat. Add the onion and garlic and cook gently until softened but not coloured, about 10 minutes. Add the potatoes with the hot stock or water, turn the heat to medium and bring to the boil. Adjust the heat and simmer steadily until the potatoes are cooked through, about 20 minutes.

Meanwhile, make the pesto. Put the garlic, rocket and pine nuts in a food processor and pulse until finely chopped. Add the Parmesan, then, with the motor running, trickle in the oil to make a smooth paste. Taste and adjust the seasoning.

Put the soup with the cream or goat's cheese in a food processor and pulse to a silky smooth purée. Return the soup to the rinsed out pan, thin with hot water as needed, and reheat gently until piping hot, but not boiling. Add salt and pepper to taste.

Ladle the soup into warmed bowls and serve hot, each portion of soup topped with a generous spoonful of rocket pesto.

THINK AHEAD
You can make the pesto several days ahead; keep covered and chilled. The soup can be made a day ahead; cool completely before covering and chilling.

CELERIAC & APPLE SOUP
WITH BACON & CABBAGE

This is a bonus recipe - which didn't appear in the original edition of *Books for Cooks 4*. When we came to reprint, we found we had a page spare, and, since this little volume was always quite light on soups, we thought we might as well throw in this new test kitchen favourite, courtesy of Eric.

SERVES 4

30 g (1 oz/2 tbsp) butter
1 tbsp olive oil
1 onion, finely chopped
2 cloves garlic, finely chopped
1 carrot, chopped
2 apples, chopped
1 medium celeriac, chopped
1 medium potato, chopped
1 litre (1 ¾ pints/4 cups hot stock or water
salt, black pepper
4 rashers of streaky bacon, rind removed, chopped
¼ Savoy cabbage, cored and finely shredded

MELT THE BUTTER with the oil in a pan over a low heat. Add the onion, garlic and carrot and cook gently until softened but not coloured, about 10 minutes. Add the apples, celeriac and potato with the hot stock or water, turn the heat to medium and bring to the boil. Adjust the heat and simmer steadily until the potato is cooked through, about 20 minutes.

Put the soup in a food processor (you may have to do this in batches) and pulse until silky smooth. Return the soup to the rinsed out pan over a medium, thin with hot water as needed, and reheat until simmering. Add the bacon and cabbage and simmer gently until the cabbage is bright green and tender, about 15 minutes. Add salt and pepper to taste.

Ladle the soup into warmed bowls and serve hot.

Main Courses

INDONESIAN MARINATED CHICKEN WITH ROAST SWEET POTATOES & PEPPERS

A complete meal-in-itself-dish - we love its bright, bold flavours and colours. It's a particular favourite of Victoria's when cooking at home for friends or family. She likes to arrange everything on a large warm platter, pop it in the middle of the table and let everyone dig in and help themselves. Her favourite presentation is to arrange the chicken in the centre of the platter, the roasted vegetables piled down one side, and place a large bowl of yoghurt on the other.

SERVES 4

8 organic chicken thighs

FOR THE MARINADE
1 onion, quartered
2 ½ cm (1 inch) piece of fresh ginger
2 tbsp runny honey
6 tbsp light soy sauce
2 tbsp sambal olek (Indonesian hot chilli paste – see ingredients note
     below)
juice of 2 limes

FOR THE POTATOES
3 sweet potatoes
1 red onion
2 red peppers
2 garlic cloves, crushed
1 tbsp olive oil
1 tbsp balsamic vinegar
salt, black pepper

125 ml (4 fl oz/½ cup) thick creamy yoghurt to serve
fresh coriander (cilantro) sprigs to garnish

HEAT THE OVEN to 200 C (400 F) Gas 6.

For the marinade, put the onion, ginger, honey, soy, sambal olek and lime into a food processor and pulse to a coarse paste. Pour this sticky marinade over the chicken, turning to coat each piece well. Cover and set aside while you prepare the vegetables.

Cut the potatoes, onion and peppers into similar sized chunks. Place in a baking dish with the garlic, oil and vinegar. Sprinkle with salt and pepper and toss well so that every vegetable surface is well coated. Roast until tender and slightly caramelised, about 40 minutes.

Heat a heavy cast iron griddle or frying pan until very hot. Remove the chicken from the marinade and sear on all sides until well coloured. Transfer to a roasting pan, pour over the marinade and roast until cooked through, about 30 minutes.

To serve, arrange the chicken and roast vegetables on warmed plates, top with a generous spoonful of yoghurt and garnish with coriander sprigs.

INGREDIENTS NOTE
Sambal olek is a fiery hot and pungent Indonesian chilli paste made from red chillies, garlic and vinegar. Supermarkets do sell the Fox's Spices brand, but you can also buy it from Chinese and other Asian shops as well as from our neighbour The Spice Shop (see page 141). It keeps indefinitely in the refrigerator.

THINK AHEAD
You can marinate the chicken up to a day in advance; keep covered and chilled and return to room temperature before cooking.

The vegetables can be roasted ahead of time: cool, cover and store at room temperature. Reheat in a preheated 180 C (350 F) Gas 4 oven for 15 minutes.

CRISP ROAST PORK WITH FENNEL & MUSTARD LENTILS

We owe this dish to a rather jolly evening spent at Moro with all the Books for Cooks team (thank you Nessie!). Among all the delicious things we ate - and there was rather a lot of plate passing and tasting as you can imagine - this dish of roast belly of pork with its herby flavours and crispest of crunchiest cracklings was unanimously voted the absolute winner. Unsurprisingly, it has since become a regular feature in the Books for Cooks test kitchen. The Sams (Sam & Sam Clarke, chef-owners of Moro restaurant in Exmouth Market and authors of the superlative *Moro The Cookbook)* accompany their roast pork with Peas and Potatoes in Anis (see page 229 in their cookbook). Eric, in true French fashion, prefers mustard and lentils, although he has been known to ring the changes with a nice creamy mash - especially our Lemon & Mustard Mash on page 76.

SERVES 4-6

FOR THE PORK
1 tbsp fennel seeds
2 garlic cloves, chopped
1 kg (2 lb) organic pork belly in one piece, skin on and scored
1 tbsp salt

FOR THE LENTILS
1 tbsp olive oil
1 large onion, finely chopped
4 garlic cloves, finely sliced
125 g (4 oz) streaky bacon, preferably in a piece,
        rind removed, diced
350 g (12 oz/2 cups) Puy lentils
2 tbsp chopped fresh flat-leaf parsley
4 tbsp creamy Dijon mustard
salt, black pepper
2 ripe tomatoes, chopped

PRESS THE FENNEL seeds and chopped garlic all over the flesh of the belly - bottom and sides. Place the belly in a roasting tin skin side up. Dry the scored skin of the belly thoroughly with kitchen paper, then sprinkle the salt evenly and liberally all over the scored skin. Leave to stand for half an hour. This pre-salting is how you get really good crisp crackling.

Heat the oven to 220 C (425 F) Gas 7. Roast the pork for half an hour, then turn the oven down to 180 C (350 F) Gas 4 and bake for an hour and a half, when the crackling will be irresistibly crisp and golden and the meat meltingly tender. Remove from the oven and let stand for 5 minutes before carving - this is to allow the juices to settle inside the meat.

Cook the lentils while the pork is in the oven. Warm the oil in a large pan over medium heat. Add the onion, garlic and bacon and cook, stirring, until the onion has softened, about 5 minutes. Add the lentils, pour in boiling water just to cover, put on the lid, and adjust the heat so that the lentils simmer steadily but gently. Cook until the lentils are soft and thick, about 50 minutes, stirring from time to time and adding a little more water if the lentils start to dry out and stick. Stir in the mustard and parsley and add salt and pepper to taste.

Place the pork on a chopping board and cut into long slices about 2 cm ($\frac{1}{2}$ inch) thick. Divide the lentils among warmed plates and spoon over the chopped tomato. Arrange the pork on top and serve at once.

INGREDIENTS NOTE
The pork belly (and all the meat) we cook in the test kitchen comes from Rosie's family farm Sheepdrove Organic Farm. Pick up their newsletter and recipe sheets when you are next in the shop or see their website (**www.sheepdrove.com**) for more information.

THINK AHEAD
You can cook the lentils a day ahead, but don't add the mustard, parsley and seasoning until just before serving. Let cool completely before covering and chilling.

SMOKED FISH TART WITH LEMON & DILL

Feel free to ring the changes with this superlative fish tart courtesy of Victoria and Jennifer and their essential *Diva Cooking*. Possible fish substitutions include - a mixture of white fish and salmon, prawns, smoked salmon, queen scallops (or sliced king scallops); additional flavourings could be sautéed diced organic streaky bacon (2 rashers would do), ½ tbsp grainy mustard, a large pinch of cayenne pepper, 1 tbsp rinsed baby capers, or ¼ tsp paprika.

SERVES 4-6

500 g (1 lb) undyed smoked haddock, skinned and boned
30 g (1 oz/2 tbsp) butter
2 bunches of spring onions (scallions),
      cut into 2 ½ cm (1 inch) lengths
3 organic eggs, beaten
250 ml (8 fl oz/1 cup) crème fraîche or double (heavy) cream
grated zest and juice of 1 organic lemon
      (wash and scrub well if not organic)
75 g (2 ½ oz/¾ cup) freshly grated Parmesan
1 handful of fresh dill or fennel, chopped
salt, black pepper
24 cm (9 inch) shortcrust pastry case baked blind (pre-baked)
      (see pages 134-136)
2 tbsp extra freshly grated Parmesan to sprinkle

HEAT THE OVEN to 180 C (350 F) Gas 4 and put in a baking sheet to preheat.

Make the filling. Cut the fish into 2 ½ cm (1 inch) pieces. Melt the butter in a large frying pan over a medium heat, add the spring onions and cook, stirring, until slightly softened, about 3 minutes. Add the fish and cook until it turns opaque, about 2 minutes, then remove from the heat at once and allow to cool.

Beat the eggs, crème fraîche or cream, lemon zest and juice until smoothly combined. Stir in the fish, spring onions, Parmesan and dill or fennel and add salt and pepper to taste. Pour the filling into the pastry case, filling it right up to the brim. Sprinkle over the extra Parmesan, grind over a little extra pepper and put into the oven on to the hot baking sheet (a good tactic to avoid soggy bottoms). Bake until golden and just set, about 25 minutes. Transfer to a wire rack and let stand for half an hour before serving. Serve warm with salad of watercress tossed with roast cherry tomatoes and dressed with a grainy mustard vinaigrette.

SMOKED FISH TARTLETS WITH LEMON & DILL Turn to pages 134-135 and follow the instructions for making six 12 cm (5 inch) shortcrust pastry cases baked blind (prebaked). Make the filling as directed and bake the tartlets until just set, about 15 minutes.

GRILLED COURGETTE, FETA & MINT SALAD

A lovely late summer dish, when the evenings are cooler and we want something a little warming but still bursting with sunny, Mediterranean flavours. Excellent for vegetarians, it also superb side dish and will turn a simple lamb roast into a special meal. One last thing, don't despair if you can't find any fresh mint, parsley (especially flat-leaf), is delicious instead.

SERVES 4

500 g (1 lb) medium courgettes (zucchini), sliced lengthwise
5 tbsp olive oil
salt
2 red peppers, quartered and seeded
100 g (3 ½ oz) feta cheese

FOR THE DRESSING
1 clove garlic, finely chopped
1 tbsp finely chopped fresh mint
2 tbsp lemon juice
1 tsp runny honey
4 tbsp olive oil
salt, black pepper
1 red onion, finely sliced

MAKE THE DRESSING. Put the garlic, mint, lemon and honey in a large bowl and whisk until smooth. Still whisking, pour in the oil in a thin stream, to make a thick dressing. Season to taste with salt and pepper. Stir in the red onion to the dressing.

Heat a cast-iron ridged grill pan until very hot. Brush each courgette slice on both sides with olive oil and sprinkle with salt. Grill in batches until charred on both sides. You can of course use an overhead grill, but you won't get the nice black stripes on the courgettes. Place the grilled courgette slices in a bowl with dressing.

Put the pepper quarters skin side up under a hot grill and roast until charred and blistered all over. Then put them in a bowl, cover with a plate, and leave for 10 minutes while the trapped steam loosens the pepper skins so they may easily be slipped off. Cut each quarter in half and place in a bowl with the courgettes and their dressing. Toss well to coat everything thoroughly.

Arrange the salad on in 4 oven proof shallow bowls or on 1 large serving dish. Sprinkle the feta evenly over the top and place under a hot grill until the cheese is patched with brown and the salad is sizzling, about 10 minutes. Serve immediately.

THINK AHEAD
You can grill and marinate the vegetables up to 6 hours in advance.

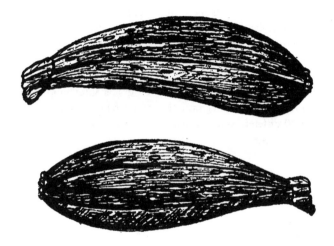

TAGINE OF MUTTON WITH CHICKPEAS

"Mutton!!?" do we hear you exclaim? "Yes, mutton!" we retort! Our little books have a modest tradition of promoting all kinds of ingredients, some new and exotic, some traditional and fallen from favour - pomegranate molasses *(Books for Cooks 1)* beetroot *(Books for Cooks 2)*, celeriac *(Books for Cooks 3)*, chipotles in adobe *(Books for Cooks 4)*, to name a few. Well, this year it's the turn of mutton to step into the spotlight.

That mutton is rarely available nowadays is a sad fact of modern farming, as farmers no longer keep their sheep in pasture for an extra year or two. With its fuller, meatier flavour than lamb, but by no means tougher texture, we think that mutton well deserves a comeback on menus both at home and in restaurants - why don't you give it a try?

If you have access to our wonderful neighbour The Spice Shop (see page 141) you can use 1 $\frac{1}{2}$ tbsp of her ras el hanout, a fabulously aromatic blend of more than 20 different spices, instead of all the different spices given in the ingredients list below.

SERVES 4

4 tbsp olive oil
2 onions, finely sliced
6 garlic cloves, crushed
1 tsp ground coriander
1 tsp ground cumin
1 tsp ground paprika
$\frac{1}{2}$ tsp ground ginger
$\frac{1}{2}$ tsp ground cinnamon
$\frac{1}{4}$ tsp chilli powder
1 kg (2 lb) shoulder of mutton, in 4 cm (1 $\frac{1}{2}$ inch) cubes
1 tbsp plain flour
2 x 400 g (14 oz) tins chopped tomatoes
250 ml (8 fl oz/1 cup) water
400 g (14 oz) tin chickpeas, drained
90 g (3 oz/$\frac{1}{2}$ cup) raisins
salt, black pepper
chopped fresh mint or coriander (cilantro) to garnish

HEAT THE OIL in a large, heavy casserole over medium heat. Add the onion and cook until softened, about 5 minutes. Add the garlic, coriander, cumin, paprika, ginger, cinnamon and chilli and cook, stirring, until spicily fragrant, about a minute.

Add the mutton with the flour, stirring until it is thoroughly coated with the spiced mixture, then cook gently until lightly browned all over, 10-15 minutes. Add the tomatoes and water, mix well and bring to a simmer. Cover and cook gently over a low heat, stirring occasionally. Or, bake for about 1¼ hours in a 160 C (325 F) Gas 3 oven.

Stir in the chickpeas and raisins and cook for a further 30 minutes. Add salt and pepper to taste. Serve hot, garnished with fresh herbs. You can serve hot buttered couscous (if you want to keep the Moroccan theme going), but a sturdy mash (see *Favourite Recipes from Books for Cooks 1, 2 & 3* and the Books for Cooks All-Purpose Mix n' Match Root Vegetable Purée on page 80) would also be good. Carrot Salad with Toasted Sesame Seeds (see page 78) adds a nice splash of fresh colour and flavour on the plate.

THINK AHEAD
Like all stews, this dish benefits from being prepared a day in advance. Let cool completely before covering and chilling. Reheat slowly as boiling the tagine hard will only toughen the meat.

INGREDIENTS NOTE Mutton is available from Rosie's parents' farm, Sheepdrove Organic Farm, which is also where our chicken comes from when we have it on the menu. See their website **www.sheepdrove.com** to know more. However, the best way to get an ingredient back in the stores is to ask for it, which we urge you to do.

SMOKEY CHIPOTLE SHREDDED PORK WRAPS WITH PINEAPPLE LIME SALSA

You don't have to serve this recipe of Jennifer's as a wrap. For a more informal, interactive dining experience, present it "chilli con carne style", in deep bowls, with all the garnishes on offer for everyone to help themselves, and plenty of warm crusty bread to hand.

For all you white meat fans out there, shredded chicken works just as well as pork. And, if pineapple doesn't take your fancy, the avocado salsa on page 48 is just the ticket.

SERVES 4

500 g (1 lb) boned organic pork shoulder
2 garlic cloves, crushed
2 onions, finely chopped
2 chipotle chillies in adobo sauce, seeded and chopped
    (see ingredients note below)
6 ripe plum tomatoes, halved
4 garlic cloves, unpeeled
1 tbsp roughly chopped fresh coriander (cilantro)
2 tbsp sunflower oil
salt, black pepper
8 flour tortillas (available from most supermarkets)

FOR THE SALSA
$\frac{1}{2}$ fresh ripe pineapple, cored and finely diced
$\frac{1}{2}$ red onion, finely chopped
juice of 1 lime
1 tbsp finely chopped fresh coriander (cilantro)

FOR THE TOPPPINGS
175 ml (6 fl oz/$\frac{3}{4}$ cup) sour cream
$\frac{1}{2}$ red onion, finely chopped
4 tbsp finely diced ripe tomatoes
fresh coriander (cilantro) sprigs to garnish

FOR THE FILLING, put the pork, 2 crushed garlic cloves and 1 of the finely chopped onions into a pan and add water to cover by 2 ½ cm (1 inch). Bring to the boil and skim off any foam. Partially cover and simmer gently until tender, about 1 ½ hours. Place the pan on a wire rack and leave the pork in its broth to cool completely. Transfer the cooled pork to a board and, using two forks, shred.

While the pork is cooling, cook the tomatoes under an overhead grill until blackened on both sides. Put the whole unpeeled garlic cloves in a small pan and cook over a medium heat until blackened all over. Cool before peeling and putting into a food processor or blender with the blackened tomatoes, the chipotle chillies and the coriander. Pulse to a roughly chopped sauce.

To make the salsa, combine the pineapple, red onion, coriander and lime. Don't do this more than 3 hours before serving, or the salsa will lose its delicious crunch.

To finish the pork, warm the oil in a frying pan and soften the remaining chopped onion, 5 minutes. Add the pork and cook, stirring, until starting to crisp, about 10 minutes. Add the blackened tomato and garlic sauce and cook for another 5 minutes to allow the flavours to blend.

Now warm the tortillas. Heat a dry frying pan and place one tortilla in the pan. Cook until warm, 15 seconds, then flip over and warm the other side. Remove from the pan and cover with a tea towel. Repeat with the remaining tortillas.

Spoon about 4 tbsp of the smoky pork on to each warm tortilla. Top with the salsa and roll up. Place 2 filled tortilla wraps on each warm plate. Drizzle over sour cream, scatter with chopped red onion and tomato dice and garnish with coriander sprigs. Serve at once.

INGREDIENTS NOTE

Just what are chipotles in adobo, do we hear you cry? Well, the chipotle part is dried jalapeno chillies that have been smoked over wood fire, the adobo part is a spicy sauce which numbers garlic, herbs, vinegar and, yes you guessed it, more chillies, among its component parts. The combination of the two is hot, smokey, and fabulously flavourful. We buy them in small jars from our neighbour The Spice Shop (see page 141). You only need one or two at a time, but simply pop the remaining chillies and sauce in a jam jar, cover with cling film, screw on the lid and store in the fridge where they seem to keep indefinitely. And what else to use them for? Try adding to dressings, marinades, or stews (they'll transform your usual chilli con carne) for a deliciously sweet smokey heat.

THINK AHEAD
You can make the pork the day before; cool, cover and chill. Reheat with a tablespoon or so of water in a frying pan over a medium heat until piping hot.

CRESPELLE WITH RICOTTA, SPINACH & ROSEMARY

Since retiring from Books for Cooks, Heidi has become a full-time Tuscan and devotes her energy to a new project, cookery holidays for food lovers, suitably entitled "Books for Cooks in Tuscany". Combining Heidi's special knowledge of the region with the culinary expertise of resident cook Olivia Greco, the aim is to export the special flavour of Books for Cooks to an idyllic Tuscan valley in the heart of *Chianti Classico* for a week of learning, cooking, eating and enjoying.

Olivia pays regular visits to Books for Cooks, flying over every other month and staying for about ten days in our cook's flat above the shop. While here, she divides her time between upstairs and downstairs, teaching cookery classes in the workshop kitchen and cooking lunch in the Test Kitchen. This dish won rave reviews when she was last in the downstairs kitchen and had customers begging for the recipe, so we thought we had better oblige.

SERVES 4

FOR THE CRESPELLE
125 g (4 oz/1 cup) plain (all-purpose) flour
½ tsp salt
2 organic eggs, beaten
250 ml (8 fl oz/1 cup) milk
30 g (1 oz/2 tbsp) butter to cook the crespelle

FOR THE FILLING
600 g (1 ¼ lb) fresh spinach or 400 g (14 oz) frozen leaf spinach, defrosted
500 g (1 lb) ricotta cheese
60 g (2 oz/½ cup) Parmesan, freshly grated
½ tsp finely chopped fresh rosemary
salt, black pepper

FOR THE SAUCE
30 g (1 oz/2 tbsp) butter
125 g (4 oz) cherry tomatoes, halved
125 ml (4 fl oz/½ cup) double (heavy) cream or crème fraîche
60 g (2 oz/½ cup) Parmesan, freshly grated

MAKE THE CRESPELLE. Sift the flour with the salt into a large mixing bowl and make a well in the centre. Whisk the eggs and milk together in a measuring jug. Pour about a third of the liquid into the well and gradually whisk in the flour to make a smooth paste. When making batters, never just chuck in all the liquid, as you'll end up with a lumpy batter, which you'll have to sieve. Pour in the remaining liquid in a steady stream, whisking all the time. Let the batter stand for half an hour.

Melt the butter in a 20 cm (8 inch) non-stick frying pan over a medium heat and, when it is foaming, pour off the excess into a bowl. Pour a small ladle of batter into the hot pan, tilting and swirling the batter so that the batter covers the whole pan. Cook until the crespelle is set and golden underneath, about a minute. Loosen the crespelle and turn with a spatula. Cook the second side for $\frac{1}{2}$ to 1 minute until golden. Repeat the whole process until you have used up all the batter, piling the cooked crespelle on top of each other to keep them moist. You need 16 crespelle - bear in mind that, when making crepes, it's usual to discard the first crepe, as it never seems to turn out right!

Make the filling. If you are using fresh spinach, wash the spinach first, then pile the leaves into a large pan, put on the lid and cook over a medium heat until the spinach starts to wilt, about 2 minutes. You don't need any water in the pan, as the water still clinging to the spinach leaves will create enough steam to cook the spinach. Now stir the spinach, put the lid back on, and continue cooking until completely wilted and tender, 1-2 minutes. Drain and cool. When cool enough to handle, squeeze lightly to remove any wateriness and chop roughly.

If you are using frozen spinach, cook the defrosted spinach in a covered pan for 5 minutes.

Place the spinach, the ricotta, Parmesan and rosemary in a bowl, mix thoroughly and add salt and pepper to taste.

Heat the oven to 180 C (350 F) Gas 4.

Lightly smear the bottom of an oven dish with butter. Divide the filling among the crespelle and roll up into cigarettes. Pack into the buttered dish with the folded-over end facing down and spoon the sauce over the crespelle to coat.

To make the sauce, melt the butter in a pan over a medium heat, add the tomatoes and cook until softened, about 5 minutes. Pour in the cream, remove the pan from the heat immediately and add salt and pepper to taste. Pour the sauce over the crespelle, sprinkle evenly with the Parmesan and bake until the crespelle are hot through and just turning crisp at the edges, about 10 minutes. Serve at once.

THINK AHEAD
Unfilled, the crespelle can be made up to 2 days ahead. Stack the crespelle in single layers separated by greaseproof paper, cover and refrigerate. Or you can fill and roll the crespelle and arrange them in the oven dish up to a day ahead; cover and chill until needed. Just before serving, make the sauce and bake as directed.

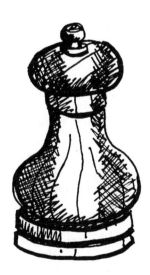

BRAISED DUCK WITH SOY, GINGER & STAR ANISE

We've been begging Victoria for this recipe for years, so we were thrilled when she included it in her and Jennifer's *Diva Cooking*. Try it and you'll see why - in fact we are pretty confident that one tiny taste of this dish will have you beating a path to your nearest bookstore for a copy of *Diva Cooking!*

SERVES 4

4 duck legs
3 cloves garlic, sliced
3 cm (1¼ inch) piece fresh ginger, cut into matchsticks
2 star anise
2 ½ tbsp sake
175 fl oz (6 fl oz/¾ cup) chicken stock
75 ml (2 ½ fl oz/⅓ cup) red wine
75 ml (2 ½ fl oz/⅓ cup) light soy sauce
½ tsp five-spice
2 tbsp runny honey
spring onions (scallions), cut into matchsticks
1 fresh red chilli, seeded and cut into matchsticks to garnish.

HEAT THE OVEN to 180 C (350 F) Gas 4.

Heat a large frying pan over low heat - no need to add any oil, the duck legs are fat enough. Add the duck legs and cook slowly until browned on both sides, about 20 minutes. Transfer the browned duck legs to a roasting pan.

Pour out any duck fat from the frying pan - keep for sautéing potatoes. Return the pan to a medium heat, add the garlic and ginger and cook until fragrant, 2 minutes. Add the star anise, sake, stock, red wine and soy, bring to the boil and let bubble briskly for 5 minutes to let the alcohol evaporate and concentrate the flavours. Your kitchen will be filled with fabulously fragrant aromas.

Pour this aromatic broth into the roasting pan. Sprinkle the duck legs with five-spice powder and drizzle with honey. Cover the roasting pan with a large piece of foil, turning over the edges to seal the pan well and making sure there are no holes or tears.

Bake until tender, about 1 hour. Turn the oven up to 200 C (400 F) Gas 6. Remove the foil from the roasting pan and return the duck to the oven to roast until the skin is nice and crispy, about 15 minutes. If the skin refuses to crisp, give the duck a quick blast under a preheated overhead grill, but keep an eye on it to avoid over browning.

Arrange the duck on warmed plates, pour over the juices and sprinkle over spring onions and chilli to garnish. Serve at once with Chicory, Watercress & Pear Salad (see page 92).

THINK AHEAD
This is a great dinner party dish as it can be made a day in advance. Cook the duck as directed, but don't bother with the final crisping. Cool the duck and juices completely before covering and chilling. When the juices are cold, you can scrape off the fat. Reheat the duck in a roasting pan covered with foil in 180 C (350 F) Gas 4 for 15 minutes, then remove the foil, and crispen as directed in the recipe.

GINGER & LIME MARINATED TIGER PRAWNS WITH AVOCADO SALSA

A pacific twist on that nowadays déclassé (but still fond favourite) combo of avocado and prawns, this looks fun, tastes fun and is fun. You don't have to serve it on a papadams, but it not only looks good, but, if you and your guests are prepared to use their hands, snapping off a crispy piece of papadam for dipping into the salsa is nice too.

SERVES 4

20 cooked peeled tiger prawns (large shrimp)
4 ready cooked papadams (Sharwoods do them)
lime wedges and fresh coriander (cilantro) sprigs to serve

FOR THE MARINADE
2 ½ cm (1 inch) piece of fresh ginger
juice and grated zest of 1 lime (preferably organic, wash and scrub well
          if not organic)
1 handful of fresh coriander (cilantro)
1 garlic clove
1 fresh red chilli, seeded
1 tsp salt
1 tbsp olive oil

FOR THE SALSA
1 avocado, finely chopped
½ red onion, finely chopped
1 handful of fresh coriander (cilantro), finely chopped
juice of 1 lime
1 tbsp olive oil
salt, black pepper

FOR THE MARINADE, put the ginger, lime, coriander, garlic, chilli, salt and oil in a food processor and pulse until blended. Combine the marinade and the prawns, stirring gently to coat each prawn well. Cover and refrigerate for 1 hour.

Meanwhile, make the salsa. Combine avocado, onion, coriander, lime and oil and add seasoning to taste.

To serve, place 1 papadam on each plate. Spoon some salsa on to the centre of each papadam, heaping it up nicely. Arrange 5 marinated prawns prettily on top. Decorate with lime wedges and coriander sprigs and serve at once.

THINK AHEAD
You can marinade the prawns up to 2 hours in advance. You can also make the marinade itself the day before and keep covered and chilled.

The salsa can be made up to 6 hours ahead. Cover and chill, making sure you press cling film directly on to the surface of the salsa. It's the oxygen in the air that turns avocado brown, so the less air that comes into contact with the salsa, the better.

BEEF & CHORIZO PIE

We found this truly excellent pie in Julie Le Clerc's *More Simple Café Food*. It boasts both a richly aromatic meat filling with fashionably Spanish overtones and a wonderfully light crisp pastry.

You might like to make individual pies. This recipe will make either eight really posh little pies for a several course dinner party with 250 ml (8 fl oz/1 cup) volume ramekins or six heartier servings using 350 ml (12 fl oz/1 ½ cup) pie dishes or ovenproof soup bowls. Individual pies will take from 15 to 25 minutes (depending on size) to cook until the filling is bubbling and the pastry nice and golden.

SERVES 6-8

1 tbsp olive oil
200 g (7 oz) chorizo sausage, sliced
1 kg (2 lb) organic stewing beef, cut into 2 ½ cm (1 inch) cubes
2 onions, sliced
4 cloves garlic, crushed
3 tbsp flour
3 tbsp tomato purée
½ tsp paprika
½ tsp dried thyme
4 tbsp dry sherry
250 ml (8 fl oz/1 cup) red wine
250 ml (8 fl oz/1 cup) beef, chicken or vegetable stock
salt, black pepper

FOR THE PASTRY
175 g (6 oz/1 ½ sticks) cold butter, cubed
350 g (12 oz/3 cups) plain (all-purpose) flour
1 ½ tbsp baking powder

WARM THE OIL in a wide heavy pot (with a lid) over medium heat. Add the chorizo and cook until the paprika oil runs, about 5 minutes. Scoop the chorizo out of the pot and set aside. Raise the heat to high, add the beef to the pot and fry until sealed and browned well on all sides. You'll probably need to do this in batches because, if the pan is overcrowded, the meat will steam rather than brown. Scoop the beef out of the pot and add to the bowl with the chorizo.

Add the onion to the pot (add extra oil if needed) and cook, stirring, until softened, golden and starting to brown at the edges, about 5 minutes. Add the garlic and cook for a minute longer. Stir in the flour and cook for a minute when it should have been absorbed into the meat fat and juices. Add the tomato purée, paprika and thyme and cook for another minute before returning the chorizo and beef to the pot. Stir everything well, then pour in the sherry and wine, bring just to a simmer, then add the hot stock or water. Cover and simmer gently until the meat is tender, about 1 hour (alternatively place the pot in a preheated 160 C (325 F) Gas 3 oven). Add salt (you may not need any as the sausages are salty) and pepper to taste. When the beef is tender, transfer to a bowl and leave to cool.

Meanwhile, make the pastry. Place the butter, flour, baking powder and salt in a food processor and pulse until the mixture resembles fine breadcrumbs. Add the milk and pulse until the pastry draws together. Turn it out on to a lightly floured work surface and knead briefly to form a flat round. If you don't have a food processor, do the whole thing as lightly as possible, using your fingertips to rub the butter into the flour and, when you add liquid, pinching the whole thing into a dough. Wrap in cling film and chill for half an hour.

Heat the oven to 190 C (375 F) Gas 5.

Roll out pastry until $\frac{1}{4}$ cm ($\frac{1}{8}$) inch thick. Using your upturned pie dish as a template, cut out a pastry lid about 5 cm (2 inches) larger than your pie dish. Now fill your pie dish with the cooled beef, chorizo and its sauce. Wrap the pastry around the rolling pin, lift into place and unroll loosely over the meat in the pie dish. Tuck the overhanging pastry underneath itself to make a double layer of pastry around the border of the pie. Now you can crimp (with a fork) or flute (with your fingers) around the edge of your pie.

Using a skewer, poke a hole for steam to escape during baking in the middle of the lid, wiggling the skewer to make the hole about $\frac{1}{2}$ cm ($\frac{1}{4}$ inch) across (any smaller and it risks closing up as it bakes). Brush the lid evenly with the egg glaze.

Hopefully you have some pastry trimmings left over. If you do, you can have some fun decorating your pie. We like to make pastry leaves - cut the pastry trimmings into diamond shapes, then score veins with the back of a knife - you could do hearts or stars or whatever small pastry cutter shapes you have to hand. Arrange your pastry leaves (or what you will) on top of the pie lid and brush the pastry with egg glaze again (this double glazing will make your pie crust bake to a really golden and tempting finish).

Put the pie into the oven on to the hot baking sheet and bake until the pastry is golden brown and crusty, about 40 minutes. Serve hot with a nice and creamy mash - try our Lemon & Mustard Mash on page 76 or perhaps an earthy root purée (see page 80 in *Favourite Recipes from Books for Cooks 1, 2 & 3*) - and steamed greens.

INGREDIENTS NOTE
If you can't locate any chorizo sausage (available in Spanish and Portuguese shops, good delicatessens, department store food halls and the deli counter of large supermarkets), you can usually find ready sliced chorizo along with the packets of sliced hams and salamis in supermarkets.

THINK AHEAD
You can certainly prepare the filling a day or two ahead; keep covered and chilled. The pastry too you can make the day before (wrap tightly in cling film and refrigerate), but it's easier to roll out if it's not rock hard from the fridge, so take out 10 minutes before rolling. Or, a day in advance, you can assemble the pie, then "hold" it in the fridge until ready to bake.

POMEGRANATE MARINATED CHICKEN WITH SAFFRON COUSCOUS, GRILLED AUBERGINES & POMEGRANATE VINAIGRETTE

Rosie and Victoria were treated to this delicious lunch on a lovely hot day in Jennifer's garden this summer. It was so good we just had to put it in the book.

The original inspiration for the chicken marinade came from Sam and Sam Clark's *Moro The Cookbook* - their recipe calls for duck breasts, which is also very good. As well as chicken and duck, Jennifer has also used this marinade - and these accompaniments - with lamb fillet and boned quail, both to great acclaim.

Pomegranate molasses is made by boiling the juice of sour pomegranates to a thick dark brown syrup with a distinctive sweet-sour flavour. Seek it out in Lebanese and Iranian shops or at the Spice Shop, just across the street from Books for Cooks.

SERVES 4

8 organic chicken thighs, boned
6 tbsp pomegranate molasses
2 tsp ground cinnamon
4 garlic cloves, crushed
1 pinch of ground allspice
1 aubergine (eggplant), sliced
3-4 tbsp olive oil

FOR THE VINAIGRETTE
125 ml (4 fl oz/½ cup) pomegranate molasses
juice of 1 lemon
1 garlic clove, crushed
1 tsp ground cumin
1 tsp sugar
125 ml (4 fl oz/½ cup) olive oil
salt, black pepper

53

FOR THE COUSCOUS

a pinch of saffron threads
500 g (1 lb/2 cups) couscous
350 ml (12 fl oz/1 ½ cups) hot chicken stock
30 g (1 oz/2 tbsp) butter
salt
1 tbsp finely chopped fresh coriander (cilantro)
1 tbsp finely chopped fresh mint

PUT THE CHICKEN, pomegranate molasses, cinnamon, garlic and allspice in a bowl and mix well to coat each piece of chicken evenly with the syrup and spices. Cover and let marinate at room temperature for at least 30 minutes and up to 6 hours in the fridge.

The easiest way to make the vinaigrette is to put the pomegranate molasses, lemon juice, garlic, cumin, sugar and olive oil in a jam jar, screw on the lid and shake vigorously to a thick dressing. Add salt and pepper to taste.

To make the couscous, place the saffron and couscous in a mixing bowl and pour over the hot stock. Cover with a plate and let sit for 10 minutes while the couscous softens and swells. Crumble any lumpy grains with your fingers. When you are ready to serve, melt the butter in a frying pan over a low heat, add the couscous and heat through gently, fluffing the grains with a fork. Add salt to taste and stir in the herbs just before serving.

Brush the aubergine on both sides with olive oil. Grill, on a barbecue, on a ridged cast-iron grill pan or under an overhead grill until tender and lightly charred on both sides, about 5 minutes per side. Place the aubergine slices in a bowl and gently toss with all but 4 tbsp of the vinaigrette. Add salt and pepper to taste.

Take the chicken out of its marinade and grill on a barbecue, on a ridged cast-iron grill pan or under an overhead grill. Start cooking on the skin side and grill until nicely crisp, about 7 minutes. Then turn over and continue grilling until cooked through, with no trace of pink, about 5 minutes. Sprinkle with salt and pepper. Arrange the couscous on a large platter, pile the chicken in the middle, surround with the aubergine slices and drizzle over the rest of the vinaigrette. A sprinkling of fresh parsley, coriander or mint would be nice. Serve at once.

FOR DUCK BREASTS Score the duck skin by cutting diagonal parallel slashes 1 cm (½ inch) apart through the skin to make a diamond pattern. Grill until the skin is crispy, about 5 minutes, then turn and grill for a further 8 minutes when they will still be pink, or 10 minutes for well done. Let the duck breasts rest for 5 minutes before slicing.

FOR BONED QUAIL Grill the bone side for 8 minutes, then turn and grill the skin side until cooked through with no trace of pink at the bone, another 5 minutes. You'll need 2 quails per person.

FOR LAMB FILLETS You'll need 500 g (1 lb) lamb neck fillets. Grill, turning several times to brown and cook evenly, for about 8 minutes for pink, 12 minutes for well done.

RICOTTA & TOMATO TART

With its golden crust and green herb flecked filling topped with red tomato discs, this is a very pretty tart. In the Test Kitchen, we like to make individual tartlets because they're easier to serve. We would always recommend you do the same if you're serving food plated for a formal dinner party, so we've included instructions for tartlets in the recipe. Otherwise, at home we prefer to make a whole tart, carry it triumphantly to table and cut it up in front of family and friends. Easy peasy cookery (no pastry to make, no preparation apart from slicing and mixing) from Bill Granger's excellent cookbook *Sydney Food*.

SERVES 4-6

500 g (1 lb/2 cups) ricotta
4 tbsp double (heavy) cream or crème fraîche
2 organic eggs, lightly beaten
5 tbsp grated Parmesan
1 handful of rocket (arugula) or fresh basil, leaves snipped
salt, black pepper, grated nutmeg
500 g (1 lb) puff pastry
4 firm ripe tomatoes, thinly sliced (a serrated knife is best
     for this)
1 organic egg yolk, beaten with 1 tbsp milk, to glaze

HEAT THE OVEN to 200 C (400 F) Gas 6. If you are making a whole tart, you'll need a large baking sheet at 30 by 40 cm (12 by 15 inches); if you are making tartlets, you'll need 2 baking sheets.

Place the ricotta, cream, eggs and Parmesan in a bowl and mix well until smooth, then stir in the rocket or basil. Add salt, pepper and nutmeg to taste.

Roll out the pastry on a lightly floured work surface to a rectangle about 30 by 40 cm (12 by 15 inches) and about ½ cm (¼ inch) thick.

To make a whole tart, transfer the rolled out pastry to a floured baking sheet - don't worry if your pastry rectangle is a bit longer than your baking sheet as you're going to be folding over the edges. You can, if you want, trim the edges to a straight line to make a neater tart. Spread the ricotta mixture over the pastry, leaving a 5 cm (2 inch) border. Brush the border with

56

the egg glaze. Fold over the pastry border on to the filling. Arrange the tomato slices in rows down the length of the tart. Sprinkle with salt and pepper. Brush the folded over pastry border with egg glaze, then bake until the filling is puffed up and set and the pastry crisp and golden, 30-35 minutes. Drizzle the tomato slices with olive oil.

To make tartlets, cut out 6 squares measuring 15 by 15 cm (6 by 6 inch) from the rolled out pastry. Place the pastry squares on the floured baking sheets. Divide the ricotta mixture among the squares and spread out, leaving a 2 cm (¾ inch) border. Brush the border with egg glaze. Fold over the pastry border on to the filling. Top each tart with tomato slices and sprinkle with salt and pepper. Brush the folded over pastry border with egg glaze, then bake until the filling is puffed up and set and the pastry crisp and golden, 20-25 minutes. Drizzle the tomato slices with olive oil.

Serve your tart or tartlets warm (reheat in a hot oven for 3 minutes if making ahead), with a salad - Jennifer's Leafy Salad with Gorgonzola Cheese & Honey Mustard Dressing (look back to *Favourite Recipes from Books for Cooks 1, 2 & 3* on page 79) would be nice.

THINK AHEAD
Bake the tart or tartlets up to 4 hours ahead. Reheat for 3 minutes in a 200 C (400 F) Gas 6 oven.

MEDITERRANEAN GRILLED CHICKEN SALAD WITH ROAST GARLIC & BASIL DRESSING

Truly a Mediterranean feast for friends! A favourite recipe of Victoria's, this is colourful, flavourful, in fact everything you could want for simple yet sensational celebration fare. It's a flexible recipe too; alternative or additional ingredients include sliced roast red pepper, toasted pine nuts, cherry tomato halves, radish slices, and garlic croûtons.

SERVES 4

1 red onion, finely sliced
6 sun-dried tomatoes in oil, drained
1 tin of artichoke hearts, drained and quartered
3 tbsp best black olives, pitted
125 g (4 oz) green beans, cut in half
4 skinned, boned organic chicken breasts
2 tbsp olive oil
juice of 1 lemon
salt, black pepper
4 small handfuls of tender green leaves (choose from watercress, baby spinach,
       rocket, lamb's lettuce (mâche), flat-leaf parsley leaves)
fresh basil leaves to garnish

FOR THE DRESSING
2 whole unpeeled garlic heads
1 tsp creamy Dijon mustard
1 ½ tbsp runny honey
3 handfuls of fresh basil leaves
4 tbsp red wine vinegar
10 tbsp good olive oil
salt, black pepper

HEAT THE OVEN to 190 C (375 F) Gas 5.

Make the dressing. Wrap the whole heads of garlic in foil and roast until soft, about 45 minutes. Cool slightly. Cut the roast garlic heads in half crosswise and squeeze out the soft garlic pulp from the papery skins into a food processor. Add the mustard, honey, basil and vinegar and, with the motor running, pour in the oil in a thin steady stream to make a thick green dressing. Add seasoning to taste.

Put the onion, sun-dried tomatoes, artichokes and olives in a large bowl. Blanch the green beans in boiling salted water for 2 minutes, then drain, refresh in cold water to stop the cooking and preserve their nice, bright green colour, drain again and add to the other salad ingredients.

Heat a cast-iron ridged grill pan over a medium heat. When it is very hot, lay on the chicken, pressing down well with a spatula (depending on the size of your grill pan, you may have to cook the chicken in batches). Cook for 1 minute, without turning or moving, until nicely striped with black. Turn over, press down again, and cook on the other side for a further minute. Transfer to a roasting tin, drizzle with the oil and lemon, sprinkle with seasoning and roast until cooked through, about 10 to 20 minutes, depending on size. You can serve the chicken while still warm or at room temperature. Allow to cool to the temperature at which you intend serving it before slicing across on the diagonal.

There are two ways to present this dish, both lovely. For a buffet or a kitchen supper, toss the chicken and all the vegetables with the dressing. Arrange the greens on a large serving platter, pile the salad on top and garnish with basil. For more formal entertaining, toss the vegetables in half of the dressing. Divide the salad among the plates, heaping it up nicely, arrange the sliced chicken on top, spoon over the remaining dressing and surround with a few of the green leaves.

THINK AHEAD
The dressing, salad ingredients and chicken can all be prepared and kept chilled a day ahead, but it's best to store each component of the salad separately. Be sure to let the chicken cool completely before chilling. For the fullest flavour, allow the dressing, salad ingredients and the chicken to return to room temperature before serving.

BAKED SPAGHETTI WITH AUBERGINES

Inspired by a baked spaghetti dish in Jill Dupleix's truly wonderful *Simple Food*, Eric concocted this meat-free version. Although we would never have guessed, until Jill let us in on the secret, spaghetti makes a really superior baked pasta, the thin strands crisping most crunchily at the edges.

SERVES 4

5 tbsp olive oil
1 large onion, finely chopped
4 garlic cloves, crushed
salt
400 g (14 oz) tin of Italian plum tomatoes, chopped
2 medium aubergines (eggplants), diced
½ tsp dried oregano
dried chilli flakes
500 g (1 lb) packet Italian spaghetti
4 tbsp freshly grated Parmesan
1 tbsp chopped fresh flat-leaf parsley

MAKE THE SAUCE. Warm the oil in a wide pan (with a lid) over medium heat. Add the onion and garlic with a pinch of salt and cook, stirring, until softened, about 5 minutes. Stir in the tomatoes, aubergines and oregano. Adjust the heat to low, cover and leave to stew slowly, stirring occasionally, until thick and meltingly soft, about 25 minutes. Season to taste with salt and chilli - we like it best with a little spicy bite.

Heat the oven to 200 C (400 F) Gas 5.

Cook the spaghetti in a large pot of boiling, salted water, until firm to the bite - use the instructions on the packet as a guide but start testing a couple of minutes before the suggested cooking time is up. Drain well, then add the spaghetti at once to the hot sauce and toss well until thoroughly mixed.

Check once more for seasoning, then pile the spaghetti in its sauce into a lightly oiled gratin dish or individual dishes (we use those round shallow ovenproof dishes with two handles that look like ears), sprinkle evenly with Parmesan and bake until piping hot and turning crisp on top, 5 to 10 minutes. Sprinkle with parsley and serve immediately.

THINK AHEAD

The great thing about baked spaghetti is that, unlike most pasta dishes, you can prepare the whole thing well ahead of time. Cook the spaghetti as directed. Just before draining, add a tablespoon of olive oil, give the spaghetti a thorough stir, then drain well. Refresh the spaghetti under running cold water to stop the cooking. Store in an airtight container in the refrigerator. Make the sauce as directed and let cool completely before covering and chilling. When you are ready to serve, reheat the sauce until hot through, stir in the spaghetti, transfer to the dish and bake as directed.

BAKED SPAGHETTI WITH SPICY SAUSAGE SAUCE. Turn to page 57 in *Favourite Recipes from Books for Cooks 1, 2 & 3* and make the spicy sausage sauce instead of the aubergine sauce.

CHICKEN COOKED WITH BAY, GARLIC AND WHITE WINE

Very quick, using only a handful of ingredients, and with almost zero preparation required, this robustly flavoured dish is simplicity itself. Three cheers for the very talented husband and wife duo the Sams Clark and their very wonderful first (we hope of many) cookbook *Moro The Cookbook*.

SERVES 4

4 tbsp olive oil
2 whole heads of garlic, cloves separated, skins on
8 organic chicken thighs
6 fresh or 3 dried bay leaves
200 ml (7 fl oz/¾ cup + 2 tbsp) dry white wine or Fino (dry) sherry
100 ml (3 ½ oz/⅓ cup + 2 tbsp) water
salt, black pepper

PUT THE OIL in a large, heavy-bottomed pan (it should have a lid), turn on the heat to medium high, and when the oil is hot, add the garlic cloves and cook until fragrant and starting to soften, 2-3 minutes. Scoop the garlic cloves out of the pan with a slotted spoon and set aside.

Now put in the chicken and brown well on both sides. You will need to do this in batches, because, if the pan is too full, the chicken will steam rather than fry. When all the chicken is nicely golden brown, return to the pan with the garlic. Add the bay leaves and pour in the wine. Let the wine simmer briskly for about 30 seconds to let the alcohol evaporate.

Now add the water, put on the lid and adjust the heat to a slow simmer. Cook, turning the chicken pieces in the sauce a couple of times, until tender and cooked through (check by cutting into the chicken with a small sharp knife), 15-20 minutes, depending on the size of the chicken pieces. If, while the chicken is cooking too much of the sauce evaporates, add a tablespoon or so water as needed.

Season the chicken pieces and their sauce to taste with salt and pepper and serve at once, with our Creamy Potato Gratin (see page 94) or a nice mash (look back to *Favourite Recipes from Books for Cooks 1, 2 & 3* and the All-Purpose Mix n' Match Root Vegetables Purée).

SPICY SAUSAGE & BROCCOLI TARTLETS WITH ROAST CHERRY TOMATOES

Use the best meatiest sausages you can buy for this recipe of Jennifer's - although that is easier said than done: try and find pure meat Italian or Toulouse sausages, or, at a pinch, choose Cumberland sausages as they usually have a higher meat content than regular sausages.

You can make one large and nicely rustic looking pie rather than fancier individual tartlets. Roll out pastry to 1 rough square - aim for 30 by 30 cm (12 by 12 inches) - and transfer to a floured baking sheet - don't worry if your pastry is a bit wider than your baking sheet as you'll be folding over the edges. Now fill the pie (turning over the pastry edges) and bake as directed, allowing about 35 minutes baking time.

SERVES 4

175 g (12 oz) puff pastry (about half a packet - freeze the other
     half for the next time you make the recipe)
300 g (10 oz) sprouting broccoli, broccoli di rapa, or broccoli
3 tbsp olive oil
350 g (12 oz) best meaty pork sausages, skinned
1 garlic clove, finely chopped
$\frac{1}{2}$ tsp fennel seeds
$\frac{1}{4}$ tsp crushed chilli flakes
12 (about 200 g (7 oz)) ripe cherry tomatoes, halved
salt, black pepper
4 tbsp freshly grated Pecorino or Parmesan
125 g (4 oz) mozzarella, diced
1 tbsp balsamic vinegar
1 handful fresh basil, torn
extra olive oil to serve

HEAT THE OVEN to 200 C (400 F) Gas 6. Have ready 2 floured baking sheets.

Roll out the pastry on a lightly floured surface to a square about 30 by 30 cm (12 by 12 inches). Cut out four equal-sized squares from the rolled out pastry. You can, if you want, trim the edges straight to make neater pies. Place the pastry squares on the floured baking sheets and chill until needed.

Cut up the broccoli into 2 ½ cm (1 inch) pieces and cook in a pan of boiling salted water until just tender, from 2 to 4 minutes. Drain and straightaway refresh the broccoli pieces in plenty of cold water to preserve their nice fresh green colour, then drain well.

Warm the oil in a large frying pan over a medium high heat. Stir in the sausage meat, garlic, fennel and chilli. Fry quite briskly, stirring and squashing with a wooden spoon to break up the sausage meat into pieces, until nicely browned, about 5 minutes. Stir in the broccoli pieces and cherry tomato halves and cook for another minute to flavour with the herby, spicy oil. Add salt, pepper and any extra chilli to taste.

Divide the sausage mixture among the pastry squares, leaving a 2 cm (¾ inch) border, aiming to have a few of the tomato halves on top for the best colour, then sprinkle over the grated cheese. Fold over the pastry border on to the filling, pleating as you go.

Bake the tarts until the pastry is crisp and golden, 20 to 25 minutes, swapping the baking sheets over half way through baking. Transfer each pie to a warmed plate, sprinkle with mozzarella dice, drizzle with the balsamic vinegar and olive oil, grind over a little pepper and scatter with basil. Serve at once. We suggest crisp green salad dressed with Ursula's Lemon and Parmesan Dressing (see page 87).

THINK AHEAD
You can assemble the tarts several hours before serving and then "hold" in the refrigerator until needed - let the spicy sausage mixture cool completely before using it to fill the pastry. Or you can bake the tarts a day ahead and reheat for 5 minutes in a hot oven.

CHORIZO & SWEET POTATO SALAD

All right, so none of the ingredients in this recipe are exactly everyday common pick-it-up-at-the-corner-shop sort of ingredients, at least not here in Britain. But, once you've succeeded in tracking them down, this recipe is so quick and easy and the fabulous flavour combinations - starchy sweet plus meaty spice plus peppery greens - so delicious that we can guarantee you won't regret going to all that trouble shopping.

We owe its creation to Jill Dupleix and we found it in her *Simple Food*. It makes a great light lunch/supper dish as well as a really brightly coloured and boldly flavoured first course. We recommend choosing white plates for serving; you'll find that white shows off the brilliant colours - orange, red and green - of this sensational salad to best advantage.

SERVES 4

500 g (1 lb) sweet potatoes (about 3),
olive oil for brushing
300 g (10 oz) chorizo sausage
1 tbsp lemon juice
2 tbsp olive oil
1 tbsp parsley
4 handfuls of rocket (arugula) leaves
salt, black pepper

HEAT THE OVEN to 200 C (400 F) Gas 6. Cut the sweet potatoes into 1 $\frac{1}{2}$ cm ($\frac{1}{2}$ inch) thick slices slightly on the diagonal. Spread the sweet potato slices in a single layer on a baking sheet and brush with olive oil. Bake until patched with brown and tender when pierced with the tip of a knife, about 10 minutes on each side.

While the potato slices are roasting, cut the chorizo into 1 $\frac{1}{2}$ cm ($\frac{1}{2}$ inch) thick slices slightly on the diagonal. Heat a large frying pan over medium heat. Add the chorizo slices and fry until crisp and sizzling on both sides, about 5 minutes. Put the chorizo slices in a large bowl and pour over the paprika-tinted oil released during frying. Add the sweet potato slices with the lemon, olive oil and parsley and mix gently.

Divide the rocket among four plates. Top with the sweet potatoes and chorizo and drizzle over any dressing left in the bottom of the bowl. Sprinkle with salt and pepper and serve at once.

MONKFISH, BACON & ROSEMARY SKEWERS WITH LEMON ANCHOVY DRESSING

A mini version of these elegant skewers featured in Eric and Victoria's superlative *Canapés* cookbook. Supermarket packets of rosemary were fine for those dainty fish sticks, but for these man-sized main course skewers, though, you really need a well-established rosemary bush in your garden, or access to the Portobello Road, or another decent market, or proper green grocer. If none of these options are available, don't despair: you can still make smaller skewers with supermarket sized sprigs, allowing 3 per person, or simply use bamboo or metal skewers instead.

SERVES 4

350 g (12 oz) monkfish tail, filleted and skinned
3 slices of streaky bacon, rind removed
4 x 15 cm (6 inch) rosemary sprigs
salt, black pepper
lemon wedges to garnish

FOR THE DRESSING
4 anchovy fillets
a saucer of milk
juice of 1 lemon
100 ml (3 ½ fl oz/7 tbsp) olive oil
1 tbsp crème fraîche

CUT THE MONKFISH into sixteen 2 ½ cm (1 inch) cubes. Cut the bacon into 16 squares. Make the rosemary skewers by stripping the leaves off the rosemary sprigs, leaving just a nice tuft of leaves at one end. Keep the stripped leaves to make the dressing. Sharpen the non-leafy end of each skewer into a point with a small sharp knife. Thread alternate pieces of fish and bacon on to each skewer. Sprinkle with salt and pepper.

Make the dressing. Soak the anchovies in milk for 5 minutes – this rather softens the anchovies' potency so you'll find that even people who profess not to like anchovies will love this dressing. Finely chop 2 tbsp of the stripped rosemary leaves. Drain the anchovy fillets, discarding the milk, and put the anchovies with the rosemary in a food processor. With the motor running, drizzle in first the lemon, then the oil, in a slow steady stream. Lastly add the crème fraîche. Taste for seasoning, adding more lemon if necessary.

Cook the skewers on a very hot cast-iron griddle or under an overhead grill until cooked through, about 2-3 minutes on each side. If you are using an overhead grill, make sure that the rosemary-tufted ends of the skewers protrude from the oven so as not to catch fire.

Serve at once, with the lemon anchovy sauce and, as accompaniments, something green and something crunchy. In the spring and summer, we recommend steamed green beans and whole new potatoes roasted with garlic and sea salt; in the winter, we prefer wilted spinach and diced potatoes sautéed in butter and olive oil.

THINK AHEAD
You can skewer the fish and make the sauce up to 6 hours in advance; keep covered and chilled.

ROAST PUMPKIN & CHICKPEA SALAD WITH SUN-DRIED TOMATO DRESSING

We weren't surprised to read in *Simple Café Food* that this gorgeous salad has become something of a signature dish at author Julie Le Clerc's Garnet Road Foodstore in New Zealand. With its combination of sweet, slightly caramelised squash, gutsy sweet-sour dressing and nutty chickpeas, this is, in our view, salad perfection, colour, flavour and texture-wise. The dressing alone is to die for and can easily be elevated to dip status and served solo with vegetable sticks or pita crisps as dippers.

When it comes to choosing pumpkins or winter squash, don't be deceived by appearances! The nicest looking squash or pumpkins are not usually the greatest tasting - large orange skinned Jack O' Lantern pumpkins are better for carving than eating, while Turban squash with their great shape and pretty stripes also make better decorations than dinners. Butternut squash are quite readily available and, by squash standards, fairly easy to peel and cut up. As a general rule, expect about 350 g (12 oz) peeled and seeded flesh from 500 g (1 lb) whole pumpkin or squash.

SERVES 4

1 kg (2 lb) orange-fleshed pumpkin or butternut squash, cut into
    2 cm (¾ inch) cubes.
2 tbsp olive oil
400 g (14 oz) tin chickpeas, drained, or 125 g (4 oz) dried
    chickpeas, soaked overnight
2 tbsp finely chopped fresh coriander (cilantro) or mint
4 handfuls (about 150 g (5 oz)) of rocket, watercress or
    baby spinach, or a mixture

FOR THE DRESSING
6 sun-dried tomatoes
3 tbsp red wine vinegar
3 garlic cloves
1 tbsp balsamic vinegar
6 tbsp extra virgin olive oil

1 tsp sugar
1 pinch of dried chilli flakes
salt, black pepper

PREHEAT THE OVEN to 190 C (375 F) Gas 5.

Spread the pumpkin or squash in a baking dish, drizzle over the oil and toss to coat each cube evenly with oil. Roast until the pumpkin is tender and just turning brown and crusty at the edges, about 40 minutes. Leave to cool.

If you are using dried chickpeas, drain the chickpeas from their soaking water, place in a pan and add fresh water to cover. Bring to the boil and cook until tender, about 50 minutes.

While the pumpkin is roasting, make the dressing. Put the sun-dried tomatoes with the red wine vinegar in a small pan and heat through. Remove from the heat just before simmering point, cover and leave the tomatoes to soak and soften in the vinegar for half an hour. Put the sun-dried tomatoes with the vinegar, garlic, balsamic vinegar, oil, sugar and chilli flakes in a food processor and pulse to a thick, chunky dressing. Add salt and pepper to taste and adjust the flavour as needed, adding more olive oil, balsamic vinegar or sugar to taste.

For maximum flavour, it's best to add the chickpeas to the dressing while still hot. So, if using dried chickpeas, have the dressing ready to toss with the chickpeas after draining. If using tinned, bring the drained tinned chickpeas just to the boil in a pan of fresh water, then drain and add straightaway to the dressing with the pumpkin or squash cubes. When you are ready to serve, add the herbs to the dressed salad and mix gently to evenly combine. Arrange your choice of green leaves on plates, pile over the salad and serve immediately.

THINK AHEAD
You could dress the chickpeas and pumpkin or squash a day in advance. Keep covered and chilled, but return to room temperature before serving.

GRILLED LEG OF LAMB
WITH ANCHOVY, PROSCIUTTO & PARSLEY

Our favourite summer sunny Sunday lunch - this robustly flavoured recipe of Eric's takes the statutory roast out into the sunshine, but, if it rains, we don't care, as it works just as well cooked under an overhead grill.

But what about mint sauce, do we hear you say? Well, try salsa verde. This is unquestionably up there with our "we can't live without" top sauces (along with Thai sweet chilli, Cumberland, and, I'm sorry but it just has to be, Béchamel). And it also makes a great dressing for potatoes, which allows us to complete this new look at that classic British triumvirate of roast lamb, mint sauce and spuds.

Any good butcher will butterfly your leg of lamb for you, but it's quite easy and rather satisfying to do yourself. If you'd like to try your hand at it, there are excellent step-by-step, how-to photos in Eric and spice lady Brigit Erath's sumptuous *Barbecue - Where There's Smoke There's Flavour*. Or, you might like to come along to one of Eric's Lamb workshops and see him do it in the flesh, so to speak.

SERVES 4-6

FOR THE SALSA VERDE
2 handfuls flat-leaf parsley
10 fresh basil leaves
10 fresh mint leaves
1 garlic clove, crushed
1 tbsp creamy Dijon mustard
1 tbsp drained capers
2 anchovy fillets
½ tsp red wine vinegar
150 ml (5 fl oz) olive oil
salt, black pepper

FOR THE PASTE
60 g (2 oz) prosciutto
6 anchovy fillets
1 handful flat-leaf parsley
2 garlic cloves
1 tbsp balsamic vinegar

FOR THE LAMB
2 kg (4 lb) leg of organic lamb, butterflied
2 tbsp balsamic vinegar for drizzling during cooking
salt, black pepper

FOR THE POTATOES
600 g (1 ¼ lb) unpeeled evenly sized new potatoes
2 tbsp salsa verde (see recipe above)

FOR THE SALSA, place the parsley, basil, mint, garlic, mustard, capers, anchovy, vinegar and oil in a food processor and pulse until smooth. Add salt and pepper to taste. Cover and let stand for 30 minutes at room temperature to allow flavours to blend.

Put the prosciutto, anchovies, parsley, garlic and vinegar in a food processor and pulse to a smooth paste. Place lamb skin side down. With a sharp knife, cut 1 cm (¹/₂ inch) deep slits across the lamb about 5 cm (2 inch) apart. Then push the paste deep into the slits. Insert two 33 cm (14 inch) flat metal skewers diagonally from opposite corners through the butterflied lamb - this will make it easier to turn over and manoeuvre, especially if you're cooking it on the barbie.

To make your Potato Salad with Salsa Verde Dressing, cook the potatoes in plenty of boiling salted water until tender when tested with the tip of a sharp knife, about 15-20 minutes, depending on size. It's a good idea to use even-sized potatoes, whether larger or smaller, so that they take roughly the same time to cook through. When just cool enough to handle (or use rubber gloves) peel off the skins. (This is less hassle than it sounds as new potatoes are actually much less fiddly to peel when cooked than raw, especially the little ones). Add the still hot, peeled potatoes to the 2 tbsp salsa verde, stirring to coat each potato thoroughly. Taste to adjust the seasoning. Serve hot, warm or at room temperature - warm is our preference.

Preheat your barbecue or overhead grill. If you're using a grill (broiler), arrange the lamb on a wire rack roasting tin or oven tray. Cook the lamb, turning once, for 15 minutes per side for medium rare or 20 minutes per side for well done - drizzling balsamic vinegar on both sides once or twice during cooking. Remove to a board, cover with foil and leave to rest for 10 minutes before slicing. Sprinkle with salt and pepper, then cut into slices and serve warm with the remaining salsa verde and the potatoes.

THINK AHEAD
The salsa can be made several days ahead, although it's best to add the vinegar not more than an hour or two before serving to preserve the salsa's fresh green colour. Keep covered and chilled, but bring to room temperature before serving. The paste can be made a couple of days in advance and the lamb can be stuffed with the paste up to a day in advance; wrap in cling film and refrigerate.

Salads & Sides

LEMON & MUSTARD MASH

A creamy mash brimming with lively flavours that will brighten up any cold weather comfort fare.

SERVES 4

1 kg (2 lb) potatoes, halved
60 g (2 oz/4 tbsp) butter
grated zest of 1 organic lemon
     (wash and scrub well if not organic)
1 tbsp lemon juice
2 tbsp grainy mustard
4 tbsp double (heavy) cream
milk
salt, black pepper, grated nutmeg

PUT THE POTATOES in a large pan of cold salted water. Bring to the boil and, with the lid on, simmer steadily (rather than boiling hard) until tender - check after 20 minutes. Drain and then put back in the dry pan over a low heat to steam out any wateriness. Using either a food mill, an electric mixer, (but not a food processor or you'll get wallpaper paste) or sheer muscle power, mash to a smooth purée. Then beat in the butter, lemon zest and juice, mustard and cream, drizzling in a little milk as needed to achieve the consistency of a thick purée. Keep beating until the potatoes are really light and fluffy. Season to taste and serve at once.

LEMON, MUSTARD & SPRING ONION MASH Finely slice a bunch of spring onions (scallions). Make the mash as directed and beat in the spring onions.

LEMON, MUSTARD & CARROT MASH Make the mash as directed and beat in 1 freshly grated carrot.

LEMON, MUSTARD & PARSLEY MASH Make the mash as directed and beat in a handful of chopped fresh flat-leaf parsley.

CHICKPEA CHILLI YOGHURT SALAD

A heavenly combination of nutty pulses and bright fresh flavours make this unquestionably the best chickpea salad in the world. We owe this light but nutritious first course or side dish to the super-talented Julie Le Clerc and her *More Simple Café Food*.

SERVES 4

2 - 400 g (14 oz) tin chickpeas or 200 g (7 oz) dried chickpeas,
    soaked overnight
1 fresh red chilli, seeded and finely chopped
1 red pepper, cut into fine dice
grated zest and juice of 1 organic lemon
    (wash and scrub well if not organic)
2 tsp celery seeds
1 handful of fresh coriander (cilantro), finely chopped
1 handful of fresh mint, finely chopped
1 handful of fresh dill or fennel, finely chopped
3 spring onions (scallions), finely chopped
about 175 ml (6 fl oz/ ¾ cup) thick creamy yoghurt
salt, Tabasco
4 handfuls salad leaves

FOR THE CHICKPEAS, if using dried, drain from their soaking water, place in a pan, add fresh water to cover, bring to the boil and cook until tender, about 1 hour, then drain and let cool; if using tinned, drain and rinse well under running cold water.

In a large mixing bowl, combine the chickpeas, chilli, red pepper, lemon zest and juice, celery seeds, coriander, mint, dill or fennel and spring onions. Mix in about three-quarters of the yoghurt and add the remainder as needed - the chickpeas should be coated, not swimming, in the herby dressing. Add salt to taste and a drop or two of Tabasco if you feel the salad needs a little more heat. Chill before serving on a bed of salad leaves.

THINK AHEAD
You can certainly make the salad a couple of days ahead but chop and add the spring onions and herbs on the day of serving.

CARROT SALAD WITH TOASTED SESAME SEEDS

From *Avoca Café Cookbook* by Hugo Arnold with Leylie Hayes. The quality of your carrots will make or break this salad. Be prepared to touch as you shop and avoid carrots that feel limp or wrinkled. Also, there's no question about it, for truly great carrot salads, choose organic. On the flavour front, organic carrots win every time. The reason is simple: they contain less water. And, you don't even have to peel them, so you get more carrot, nutrient and fibre (and less water) for your pennies.

SERVES 4

1 tbsp sesame seeds
350 g (12 oz) carrots (that's 4-6 carrots), coarsely grated

FOR THE DRESSING
1 garlic clove, crushed
2 tsp runny honey
2 tsp creamy Dijon mustard
2 tbsp red wine vinegar
2 tbsp olive oil
3 tbsp sunflower oil
salt, black pepper

FOR THE DRESSING, place the garlic, honey, mustard and vinegar in a salad bowl and whisk until smooth. Still whisking, slowly trickle in the 2 oils to make a thick creamy dressing. Add salt and pepper to taste.

Toast the sesame seeds in a dry pan over medium heat until golden brown and nuttily aromatic, 3-5 minutes.

Add the carrots and sesame seeds to the dressing and toss well to evenly distribute the dressing and the seeds. Serve at room temperature.

THINK AHEAD
You can make the dressing several days ahead. Put all the ingredients in a jam jar, put on the lid, shake vigorously to combine and refrigerate (you'll need to shake or whisk to re-emulsify before using).

The carrots can be grated up to a day ahead; store in an airtight container in the refrigerator. You can dress the salad up to 6 hours in advance, any longer and the salad gets a bit watery.

BOOKS FOR COOKS FOCACCIA
WITH GARLIC PARSLEY PESTO

All you need is one great bread dough and a whole world of flavoured breads opens up. We make this focaccia dough everyday in the kitchen and simply add flavourings and toppings to ring the changes according to season and fancy.

SERVES 8

FOR THE DOUGH
500 g (1 lb/ 3 ½ cups) strong white (all-purpose) flour
2 tsp salt
325 ml (11 fl oz/1 ⅓ cups) tepid water
2 tsp dried yeast
1 ½ tbsp olive oil

FOR THE TOPPING
100 ml (3 ½ fl oz/⅓ cup + 2 tbsp) olive oil
1 handful of fresh flat-leaf parsley
4 garlic cloves,
½ tsp salt
¼ tsp black pepper

PUT THE FLOUR in the bowl, make a well in the middle and put the salt on a raised ridge of flour around the sides. Pour the water into the well and sprinkle over the yeast. Leave for 5 minutes to soften, and then stir to dissolve. Draw in enough of the flour to make a soft paste. Cover with a cloth and leave to "sponge" for 20 minutes until bubbly and slightly puffed up.

Add the oil and draw in the rest of the flour to make a rough dough. This is quite a sticky dough but try to resist working in too much extra flour as you knead. Remember the golden rule of bread making - "wetter is better"!!! Moist dough will bake to a light bread with a crisp crust and an airy crumb, while stiff dough makes heavy bread.

Turn out on to a lightly floured surface and knead until smooth, light and elastic, about 10 minutes. Put back into the bowl, cover with a cloth and leave until doubled in size, about 1 ½ hours.

Deflate the dough by pressing down with the palm of the hand. Roll out to a flat round about 23 cm (9 inch) across and place on a floured baking sheet. With your fingertips, dimple the dough all over, making dents about 1 cm ($\frac{1}{2}$ inch) deep. Cover with a cloth and leave to raise for about 20 minutes while you heat the oven to 200 C (400 F) Gas 6.

Make the pesto. Put the oil, parsley, garlic, salt and peper in a measuring jug and whiz to a rough purée with a hand-held blender; if you don't have a hand-held blender, use the pulse button on a food processor.

Bake the focaccia until golden, crusty and hollow-sounding when tapped underneath, 35 to 45 minutes. Transfer to a wire rack and drizzle immediately and lavishly with the pesto. Serve warm or at room temperature, cut into wedges.

BOOKS FOR COOKS SPICY FOCACCIA Add $\frac{1}{2}$ tsp dried chilli flakes and 1 tsp dried oregano to the dough with the oil.

BOOKS FOR COOKS SESAME FOCACCIA Sprinkle 1 tbsp sesame seeds evenly over the dough with $\frac{1}{2}$ tsp salt. When baked, drizzle with 2 tbsp olive oil.

BOOKS FOR COOKS LEMON FOCACCIA Cut half an organic lemon (wash and scrub well if not organic) into fine slices. Arrange the slices prettily over the dough before sprinkling with $\frac{1}{2}$ tsp salt.

THINK AHEAD
We generally make our focaccia dough the day before and leave to rise slowly overnight in the refrigerator. In fact we feel that the dough benefits from this slow rising. Do remove the dough from the fridge about 2 hours before shaping and baking so that it has time to return to room temperature.

FOCACCIA WITH ROAST RED ONIONS

This luscious focaccia, glistening with dark, sweet roasted onions and golden molten cheese is the one you are most likely to see adorning the test kitchen counter. You can also find the recipe in Ursula and Eric's collaborative *tour de force,* the very wonderful and, we fiercely maintain, totally essential *Bread*.

SERVES 8

FOR THE DOUGH
1 quantity of BOOKS FOR COOKS FOCACCIA dough, mixed, kneaded
    and risen as directed for about 1 ½ hours (see page 80 for ingredients
    and method).

FOR THE TOPPING
125 g (4 oz) Gruyère
3 red onions, each cut into 8 wedges
1 tsp salt
½ tsp black pepper
3 sprigs of fresh thyme, leaves stripped
2 tbsp olive oil
2 tbsp extra olive oil for drizzling

Deflate the dough by pressing it down with the palm of your hand. Roll out to a round about 23 cm (9 inch) across and place on a floured baking sheet. Spread first with cheese, then with onions. Cover with a cloth and leave to rise for about 20 minutes while you heat the oven to 200 C (400 F) Gas 6.

Sprinkle the onions with salt, pepper and thyme, then drizzle over the oil. Bake the focaccia until golden, crusty and hollow-sounding when tapped underneath, 35 to 45 minutes. Transfer to a wire rack and drizzle immediately with the extra olive oil. Serve warm or at room temperature, cut into wedges.

POTATO FOCACCIA WITH THYME, GRUYÈRE & CRÈME FRAÎCHE

This potato bread makes a rather unusual but mighty popular alternative starchy side dish for stews and braises, while, served with Roast Tomatoes (see page 93) and a green salad, it's lovely luncheon fare.

SERVES 8

FOR THE DOUGH

1 quantity of BOOKS FOR COOKS FOCACCIA dough, mixed, kneaded and risen as directed for about 1 ½ hours (see page 80 for ingredients and method).

FOR THE TOPPING

500 g (1 lb) waxy potatoes
125 g (4 oz) Gruyère, grated
4 tbsp crème fraîche
salt, black pepper
2 tbsp fresh thyme leaves

While the dough is rising, prepare the topping. Cut the potatoes into ½ cm (¼ inch) slices. Bring a pan of salted water to the boil, add the potatoes, bring back to the boil and cook until the centres are just tender when pricked with the tip of a sharp knife, about 5 minutes. Drain well and cool.

Deflate the dough by pressing down with the palm of your hand. Roll out to a flat round about 23 cm (9 inch) across and place on a floured baking sheet. Spread first with half the cheese, then arrange the potatoes on top of the cheese. Cover with a cloth and leave to rise for 20 minutes while you heat the oven to 200 C (400 F) Gas 6.

Dot teaspoonfuls of crème fraîche on to the potatoes, scatter the remaining cheese on top and sprinkle with salt, pepper and thyme. Bake until the potato topping is crisp and golden and the bread is hollow-sounding when tapped underneath, 35 to 45 minutes. Transfer to a wire rack to cool, then serve warm or at room temperature, cut into wedges.

OLIVE BREAD WITH ONION JAM

This new creation of Ursula's was premiered this July at the first of Eric and Ursula's culinary double-act demonstrations at Books for Cooks.

This is definitely the bread to choose when baking to impress, although its rather rustic appearance initially belies its swirly prettiness once sliced.

SERVES 8

FOR THE DOUGH
1 quantity of BOOKS FOR COOKS FOCACCIA dough, mixed, kneaded and risen as directed for about 1 ½ hours (see page 80 for ingredients and method).

FOR THE FILLING
4 red onions, chopped
½ tsp salt
2 fresh bay leaves (or 1 dry)
½ tsp finely chopped fresh rosemary
4 tbsp soft brown sugar
2 tbsp red wine vinegar
black pepper
75 g (2 ½ oz/1 cup) pitted black olives

FOR THE TOPPING
3 sprigs of rosemary, leaves stripped
½ tsp coarse salt
2 tbsp olive oil

Make the onion jam while the dough is rising. Warm the olive oil over a low heat, stir in the onions, sprinkle with salt, bay and rosemary and cook, stirring occasionally, until softened, about 10 minutes. Stir in the sugar and vinegar and cook gently, stirring from time to time, until thick and meltingly soft, about 30 minutes. Add salt and pepper to taste. Set aside to cool.

Deflate the dough by pressing it down with the palm of your hand. Roll out the dough to a rectangle about 35 cm by 20 cm (14 inches by 8 inches). Stir the olives into the onion jam then spread this onion-olive mixture evenly over the dough. Roll the dough up like a Swiss (jelly) roll. Place the rolled dough on a generously floured baking sheet. Press the dough down with the hands to flatten slightly, then dimple the dough all over with your fingertips, making dents about 1 cm (½ inch) deep. Cover with a cloth and leave to rise for about 20 minutes while you heat the oven to 200 C (400 F) Gas 6.

Scatter the dough evenly with rosemary and salt. Bake the bread roll until golden, crusty and hollow-sounding when tapped underneath, 45 to 55 minutes. Transfer to a wire rack and drizzle immediately with the olive oil. Serve warm or at room temperature, cut into slices.

MOROCCAN CARROTS

A boldly flavoured, brightly coloured salad that deliciously livens up a mezze plate and makes an ideal accompaniment to tagines and other North African or Middle Eastern influenced main courses. You'll find the original in Jennifer and Victoria's completely essential *Diva Cooking*.

SERVES 4

4 tsp sweet paprika
4 tsp ground cumin
2 garlic cloves, finely chopped
4 tbsp red wine vinegar
6 tbsp olive oil
salt, black pepper
500 g (1 lb) regular or baby carrots
2 tbsp chopped fresh flat-leaf parsley

MAKE THE DRESSING. Place the paprika, cumin, garlic and vinegar in a large mixing bowl. Whisking, pour in the oil in a thin stream to make a spiced dressing. Add salt and pepper to taste.

If you are using normal-sized carrots, cut them into sticks about 5 cm (2 inches) long and 2 cm (¾ inch) thick; if you can find baby carrots, there's no need to cut them up.

Cook the carrots in plenty of boiling salted water until just tender, 5 to 10 minutes. Drain well and straightaway add to the dressing in the bowl. Toss well to coat the carrots evenly with the spiced dressing, adding extra salt and pepper as needed. Set aside for about 4 hours to allow the carrots to marinate in the deliciously piquant dressing, or chill overnight. Stir in the parsley just before serving.

THINK AHEAD
You can certainly make the salad a couple of days ahead but add the parsley on the day of serving.

LEMON & PARMESAN DRESSING

Ursula's signature vinaigrette. It's most delicious with crisp salad leaves, especially cos (romaine). This recipe will dress 4 large handfuls of salad leaves.

If you're a garlic lover, feel free to add a crushed garlic clove to the dressing.

SERVES 4

1 ½ tbsp lemon juice
4 tbsp fruity extra virgin olive oil
salt, black pepper
2 tbsp freshly grated Parmesan (you cannot use the pre-grated
    stuff)

Place the lemon juice in a salad bowl and whisk in the olive oil. Add salt and pepper to taste. Pile in your salad leaves and toss well to coat. Sprinkle over the Parmesan and toss again.

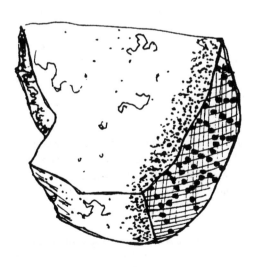

NEW POTATO, CHERRY TOMATO &
PEA SALAD WITH MINT & LEMON DRESSING

Yes, we know, another potato salad, but this one is such a useful side dish - really nice and colourful. So no apologies.

SERVES 4

350 g (12 oz) new potatoes
500 g (1 lb) fresh peas in the pod, shelled, or 250 g (8 oz)
    frozen petit pois
250 g (8 oz) cherry tomatoes, halved

FOR DRESSING
2 tbsp fresh lemon juice
5 tbsp olive oil
salt, black pepper
1 tbsp finely chopped fresh mint

MAKE THE DRESSING. Place the lemon juice in a salad bowl. Whisking, slowly trickle in the olive oil. Add salt and pepper to taste.

Cook the potatoes in plenty of boiling salted water until tender when tested with the tip of a sharp knife, about 15-20 minutes, depending on size. It's a good idea to use even-sized potatoes, whether larger or smaller, so that they take roughly the same time to cook through.

If using fresh peas, add to the pan for the last 5 minutes cooking; if using frozen peas, add for the last 2 minutes. Drain, and, when just cool enough to handle (or use rubber gloves), peel the skins from the potatoes. (This is less hassle than it sounds as new potatoes are actually much less fiddly to peel cooked than raw, especially the little ones). Leave the potatoes whole or halve or slice as necessary.

Add the still warm potatoes, peas, tomatoes and mint to the dressing and toss gently to dress well. Taste to adjust the seasoning. Serve warm or at room temperature.

You can make the salad up to 8 hours ahead, but to retain the fresh green colour of both the mint and the peas you need to a) add the mint just before serving, as the lemon juice in the dressing tends to discolour it and b) refresh the peas in cold water after draining, then drain well again before adding to the dressing with the potatoes and tomatoes.

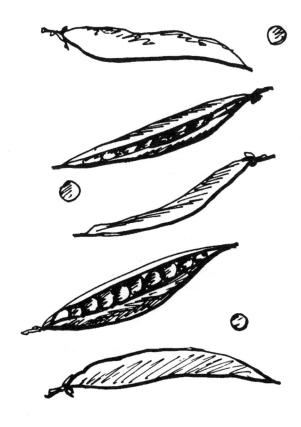

BURLGHUL SALAD WITH TOMATO, PARSLEY & POMEGRANATE

Books for Cooks devotees will be all too familiar with pomegranate molasses - hopefully *Books for Cooks 1* persuaded you to purchase your first bottle, if not, Jennifer's Pomegranate Marinated Chicken in *Books for Cooks 5* must have propelled you into action.

And, of course, now that you own a bottle, we feel quite obliged to continue supplying you with uses for this edible pet passion of ours. We've included two recipes in this little volume - this exquisite (as much to the eye as to the palate) Syrian salad from Nada Saleh's *Seductive Flavours of the Levant* and Jennifer's versatile vinaigrette on 53.

SERVES 4

1 medium red or yellow onion, very finely chopped
4 tbsp olive oil
1 ½ tsp tomato purée
1 ½ tbsp pomegranate molasses (see ingredients note below)
175 g (6 oz/1 cup + 1 tbsp) fine burghul
    (see ingredients note below)
3 tbsp water
300 g (10 oz) ripe tomatoes (about 4-5), cut into fine dice
1 ½ tsp salt
1 handful of fresh flat-leaf parsley, chopped
2 handfuls of cos (romaine) leaves
2 spring onions, sliced
seeds of 1 pomegranate

Place the onion, oil, tomato purée and pomegranate molasses in a bowl and mix well to combine. Place the burghul on top. Sprinkle the water over the burghul, spread the tomatoes in an even layer over the burghul and sprinkle with salt. Let stand for 5 minutes, then mix everything very well together. Cover and let stand for half an hour, until the burghul has absorbed all the juices and is just tender but still a little nutty. Just before serving, stir the parsley into the salad. To serve, heap the salad up on a bed of leaves and scatter with spring onion and pomegranate seeds.

INGREDIENTS NOTE

Pomegranate molasses is made by boiling the juice of sour pomegranates to a thick dark brown syrup with a distinctive sweet-sour flavour. Seek it out in Lebanese and Iranian shops or at The Spice Shop (see 141), just across the street from Books for Cooks (yes, they post too!). **Fine burghul** is also available from The Spice Shop. If you're up in the West End, it's well worth making a visit to Green Valley (at 36 Upper Berkley Street behind Selfridges) which, as well as being a regular treasury of Middle Eastern ingredients (including, of course, pomegranate molasses and fine burghul), has a wood-fired bread oven where they bake fabulous flat breads and Lebanese snacks all day long.

THINK AHEAD

You can make the salad a day ahead. Cover and chill, but add the parsley and garnish with spring onion and pomegranate just before serving.

CHICORY, PEAR & WATERCRESS SALAD

Peppery and bitter greens meet and marry perfectly with the sweetness of the
pear in this classic salad courtesy of Victoria. You needn't however restrict
yourself to watercress - try baby spinach, rocket (arugula) or lamb's lettuce
(mâche) - or chicory - try frisee (curly endive) or radiccio. The addition of
Parmesan shavings or crumbled blue cheese make this simple salad a lovely
light first course.

SERVES 4

2 ripe pears
½ red onion, finely sliced
1 ½ tbsp lemon juice
5 tbsp olive oil
salt, black pepper
150 g (5 oz/4 handfuls) watercress
1 head of chicory (Belgian endive)

CUT THE PEARS into quarters, then core and peel before cutting into thick
slices. Place the pears, onion, lemon juice and oil in a large bowl. Add salt and
pepper to taste and toss to coat the pears evenly with this simple dressing.

Separate the watercress into nice sprigs. Trim the chicory and separate into
leaves. Cut the larger leaves in half lengthwise.

Just before serving, add the leaves to the pears and toss to coat each leaf with
dressing. Serve at once.

THINK AHEAD
If well coated with the lemony dressing, the pears can be sliced and dressed
up a couple of hours ahead of time without turning brown.

ROAST TOMATOES

If supermarkets are your only source of veggies, we thoroughly recommend you buy your tomatoes well in advance. Buy plenty, buy plum (if you can, vine ripened if you can't) and set them on a tray, making sure they're not touching, near the kitchen window. They'll probably take at least several days to get up to standard. You'll be amazed at what a difference having properly ripe tomatoes makes in all your cooking.

SERVES 4

6 ripe plum tomatoes, halved
1 garlic clove
salt, black pepper
1 tbsp sherry or balsamic vinegar
1 ½ tbsp olive oil

HEAT THE OVEN to 150 C (300 F) Gas 2.

Put the tomatoes on an oven tray, cut side up. Cut the garlic clove in half and cut each half into 6 slivers. Stick a sliver of garlic into each tomato. Sprinkle each tomato with a small pinch of salt and pepper. Drizzle over the vinegar and the oil. Put into the oven to slow roast for 2 hours. You can serve them hot, warm or at room temperature, just as they are, drizzled with more olive oil or scattered with fresh herbs.

THINK AHEAD
You can roast the tomatoes a day ahead. Keep them at a cool room temperature if you can, in the fridge if you can't, returning to room temperature before serving.

CREAMY POTATO GRATIN

For total gratin success every time, follow this recipe. Eric says this is how they make potato gratins in French *bistrots* and *restaurants* - and he should know, having worked in a few.

We say waxy, rather than floury, potatoes make the best gratins; if in doubt, use new or baking potatoes.

SERVES 4

1 garlic clove, halved
15 g (½ oz/1 tbsp) butter
500 g (1 lb) potatoes, thinly sliced
250 ml (8 fl oz/1 cup) milk
125 ml (4 fl oz/½ cup) crème fraîche or double (heavy) cream
salt, black pepper, grated nutmeg
2 tbsp grated Gruyère cheese

HEAT THE OVEN to 200 C (400 F) Gas 6.

Vigorously rub the sides and base of your gratin dish with the cut side of the garlic halves, then smear the dish evenly with the butter. Put the potatoes with the remains of the crushed garlic in a pan and add the milk so that it comes just level with the top of the potatoes. Over low heat, gently bring the milk to just below simmering point, then adjust the heat so that the milk barely trembles. Cook the potatoes for 5 minutes, then remove from the heat.

With a slotted spoon, scoop the potato slices out of the pan and arrange in the garlicky buttered dish. Add the cream to the hot milk and season to taste with salt, pepper and nutmeg. Ladle the hot creamy milk over the potatoes. The liquid should come just level with the top layer of potatoes - to use Eric's words, you don't want to drown them, so you may not need it all. Sprinkle with the cheese and bake until the potatoes are tender and golden, about 45 minutes. Serve at once.

THINK AHEAD
The gratin can be baked a day in advance. Cool completely before covering and chilling. Cover with foil and reheat in a 200 C (400 F) Gas 6 oven until hot through, 15-20 minutes.

Sweet things

BOOKS FOR COOKS CHOCOLATE CAKE

When Rosie and Victoria first arrived at Books for Cooks, Alaphia Bidwell, a very brilliant cook from the Gambia, was cooking in the Test Kitchen. Every day she would bake a chocolate cake (which she learnt to make while working at a bistro in the *Marais* district of Paris) and this cake became so famous that Books for Cooks used to be known as "the place where they make that amazing chocolate cake." Luckily she gave us the recipe, so, after she departed for pastures new, we were able to carry on baking what had become known as the Books for Cooks chocolate cake. Every Saturday you'll find this legendary gateau, its luscious chocolate ganache glaze glistening, on the Test Kitchen counter. Here at last is the recipe!

SERVES 8

300 g (10 oz) dark (bittersweet) chocolate, broken into pieces
150 g (5 oz/1 stick + 2 tbsp) butter
150 g (5 oz/¾ cup) caster (granulated) sugar
5 eggs, separated
45 g (1 ½ oz/⅓ cup) plain (all-purpose) flour

FOR THE GLAZE
100 ml (3 ½ fl oz/⅓ cup + 2 tbsp) double (heavy) cream
100 g (3 ½ oz) dark (bittersweet) chocolate, broken into pieces

HEAT THE OVEN to 150 C (300) Gas 2. Butter a 24 cm (9 ½ inch) springform cake tin and line the base with baking parchment.

Melt the chocolate and the butter together in a heavy-based saucepan over very low heat, stirring constantly until smooth and glossy. Remove from the heat as soon as the chocolate has melted. Add the sugar, stir to dissolve, then leave to cool until tepid. Add the beaten yolks, a few tablespoons at a time, beating after each addition. Gently fold in the flour until just combined. Don't over mix.

Put the egg whites in a large bowl and whisk until soft peaks form - just for the record, soft peaks is when you lift up some of the egg white foam with the whisk and they will hold their shape but droop slightly when the whisk is lifted out. Use a rubber spatula to gently fold about a quarter of the beaten whites into the chocolate mixture. Add this lightened chocolate mixture to the remaining egg whites and gently fold together. Pour into the prepared tin and bake until the top is firm to the touch but a toothpick inserted in the middle comes out still moist and moussy, about 45 minutes. Place on a wire rack to cool completely.

For the glaze, heat the cream in a small pan until just below simmering point and remove at once from the heat. Add the chocolate and leave to melt for a minute or so, then stir until smooth and glossy. Leave to cool for about half an hour until slightly thickened.

When the cake has cooled completely, unmould and spread the glaze evenly over the top of the cake. You can decorate with cherries still on their stalks, strawberry halves or whole raspberries, or you might like to serve with a pool of berry coulis (whizz a handful of fresh or frozen strawberries or raspberries until smooth).

THINK AHEAD
You can bake this cake a day ahead, but keep it at room temperature rather than in the fridge. Store in an airtight container.

BLUEBERRY BUTTER CAKE

Ideal morning coffee or tea time fare from Bill Granger's gorgeous *Sydney Food*. It's the sour cream that makes this lovely cake extra moist and tender with an especially light soft crumb.

Feel free to ring the changes and use other berries (blackberries, red, white or blackcurrants, raspberries or mulberries) instead of blueberries. Frozen will do if fresh berries are not available.

SERVES 8

FOR THE TOPPING
200 g (7 oz/1 cup) soft brown sugar
4 tbsp plain (all-purpose) flour
75 g (2 ½ oz/5 tbsp) cold butter

FOR THE CAKE
250 g (8 oz/2 cups) plain (all-purpose) flour
2 tsp baking powder
¼ tsp salt
125 g (4 oz/1 stick) butter, softened
250 g (8 oz/1 cup) caster (granulated) sugar
3 organic eggs, lightly beaten
250 ml (8 fl oz/1 cup) sour cream
500 g (1 lb/2 cups) blueberries

HEAT THE OVEN to 180 C (350 F) Gas 4. Butter a 24 cm (9 ½ inch) springform cake tin and line the base with baking parchment.

Make the topping. Put the sugar, flour and butter in a bowl and either cut with 2 knives or rub with fingertips until crumbly. Or, use a food processor.

Make the cake. Sift the flour, baking powder and salt. Beat the butter and sugar together until white and fluffy. Beat in the eggs a little at a time, sprinkling in 1 tbsp of the flour when you have added about half of the beaten eggs (this is to stop curdling). Add one-third of the flour to the beaten butter-sugar-eggs mixture and fold in. Add one-third of the sour cream and fold in. Alternately add the remaining flour and sour cream until evenly combined.

Spread the batter in the cake tin and cover with an even layer of blueberries. Sprinkle the crumb topping over the blueberries. Bake until the sides of the cake have shrunk slightly away from the tin and a skewer inserted into the cake comes out clean, 40 to 50 minutes. Place on a wire rack and let cool for 15 minutes before unmoulding. You can serve it warm as a pudding or leave to cool completely and serve as a tea time treat.

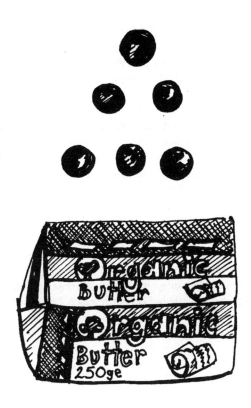

CHOCOLATE FUDGE BROWNIES

We have Deborah Sonin, baker extraordinaire, to thank this recipe, officially voted the Best Ever Brownies by Books for Cooks. Deborah (Debs to us) was born and raised in New York but, although geographically based in London, in the kitchen she sticks close to her roots, describing her style as American Jewish New York food. We regard her as world leader in cheesecake, brownie and American-style baking.

Debs' brownie allows numerous additions and variations. Try mixing in after adding the flour and just before baking any of the following - a heaped teaspoonful of best ground espresso coffee for **Mocha Fudge Brownies**, a couple of tablespoons of roughly chopped pecans, walnuts, pistachios or hazelnuts for **Nutty Fudge Brownies**, several pieces of a broken up toffee bar for **Toffee Chip Brownies,** or (and this one's a great hit at children's parties) a healthy handful of roughly crushed Smarties for **Crushed Candy Brownies.** But for the ultimate in naughty treats, bake the brownies as directed, remove from the oven, sprinkle evenly with mini-marshmallows and chocolate chips, then return to the oven just until the chocolate melts and the marshmallows start to turn golden, about 4 minutes. Fondly christened **Death by Brownies** by the Books for Cooks team, it's these wickedly luscious chocolate confections that have a starring role at our Books for Cooks staff parties.

Another great thing about this recipe is that you can bake up these brownies at least 5 days ahead, so they're a great sweet treat to have in reserve in the biscuit tin for serving with coffee, tea, as an impromptu pudding with vanilla ice cream (and perhaps a little hot chocolate sauce, do we hear you say?).

MAKES ABOUT 16 BROWNIES

125 g (4 oz) dark (semi-sweet) chocolate, coarsely chopped
125 g (4 oz/1 stick) butter
400 g (14 oz/2 cups) caster (granulated) sugar
2 tsp natural vanilla extract
4 organic eggs
125 g (4 oz/1 cup) plain (all-purpose) flour

HEAT THE OVEN to 180 C (350 F) Gas 4 (electric fan-assisted ovens should be set to 170 C). Butter the base only of a 33 x 23 cm (13 x 9 inch) baking pan – Debs prefers to use Pyrex as she finds that metal pans conduct heat over-efficiently for this recipe, but if you are using metal, be sure not to overbake the brownies.

Melt the butter and the chocolate together, either in a microwave or in a bowl over a pan of barely simmering water, then leave to cool until tepid. Add the sugar and vanilla and stir until well combined. Add the eggs one at a time, beating well after each addition. Stir in the flour until combined – there should be no white flour showing, but a few lumps don't matter; you're aiming for a consistency that is more combined than pancake (American, not crêpe) batter but less combined than muffin batter.

Bake on the middle rack of the oven until a toothpick inserted into the middle of the brownie comes out clean, 23 to 28 minutes. Your brownies will still wobble and appear undercooked, but take them out and don't be tempted to overbake or you'll compromise their lusciously gooey interior and they'll turn into cake not brownie if you do so.

Transfer the pan to a wire rack and leave to cool completely (at least 2 hours) before cutting and taking out of the pan. Cut into slices (Debs usually divides into 16 pieces) and slide the brownies out with a spatula or palette knife – you'll probably have to discard the first slice if you want all your brownies to look uniformly perfect – regard that one as a cook's treat. No extra garnish is necessary but ice cream and chocolate sauce are always welcome.

THINK AHEAD
Debs says you can make these brownies up to 5 days in advance and store in an airtight container at room temperature. We say you need a will of iron to keep them that long.

CARROT & OLIVE OIL CAKE

The best carrot cake in the world. The proof of the pudding is... so we say, bake and believe.

We are going to take this opportunity to put formally in writing our heartfelt gratitude to Celia Brooks Brown, our Books for Cooks super-talented resident vegetarian food writer and cookery teacher, for bringing this cake into our world.

SERVES 8

175 ml (6 fl oz/¾ cup) olive oil
375 g (12 oz/1 ¾ cups) caster (granulated) sugar
3 organic eggs, beaten
175 g (6 oz/1 ½ cups) plain (all-purpose) flour
1 ½ tsp baking powder
1 ½ tsp bicarbonate of soda
1 ½ tsp ground cinnamon
¾ tsp ground cloves
¾ tsp ground cardamom
¾ tsp salt
90 g (3 oz/¾ cup) chopped pecans or walnuts
375 g (12 oz) carrots, grated

FOR THE MASCARPONE ICING
125g (4 oz/1 stick) butter, softened
250 g (8 oz/1 cup) mascarpone (or use cream cheese)
2 tsp natural vanilla extract
250 g (8 oz/2 cups) icing sugar

HEAT THE OVEN to 160 C (325 F) Gas 3. Butter a 24 cm (9 ½ inch) springform cake tin and line the base with parchment paper.

Put the olive oil, sugar and eggs in a bowl and mix well to combine. Sift the flour, baking powder, soda, cinnamon, cloves, cardamom and salt into another bowl and make a well in the centre. Add the egg and oil mixture and mix in until evenly combined. Fold in the chopped nuts and grated carrots.

Pour the cake mixture into the prepared tin and bake until a skewer inserted at an angle into the centre of the cake comes out clean, about 1 hour and a half. Keep an eye on the cake during baking, especially after the first 50 minutes, as you may need to cover the tin with a baking sheet to stop the top getting too brown. When the cake is ready, transfer to a wire rack and let cool completely in its tin.

Make the mascarpone icing (this cake is so wonderfully moist and flavourful that the icing is really not essential, but it looks so pretty and is rather delicious, in a very indulgent sort of way). With a rubber spatula, beat the butter, mascarpone and vanilla together until creamy. Sift over the icing sugar and fold into the creamy mixture until completely smooth. It's best to do this by hand as overmixing in a food processor or mixer will curdle the icing.

Run a knife around the edge of the cake to loosen, then unmould. Spread the mascarpone icing on top of the carrot cake, swirling the icing decoratively.

THINK AHEAD
This fabulously moist cake can certainly be made a day ahead. Store at room temperature in an airtight container.

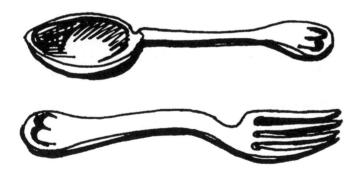

ORANGE MERINGUE CAKE

A tall crown of airy meringue tops this moist and zestily orange cake - this recipe of Olivia's is a total winner.

SERVES 8

FOR THE CAKE
150 g (5 oz/1 ¼ cups) plain (all-purpose) flour
1 tbsp baking powder
¼ tsp salt
125 g (4 oz/1 stick) butter, softened
125 g (4 oz/⅔ cup) caster (granulated) sugar
grated zest and juice of 2 organic oranges
        (wash and scrub well if not organic)
4 organic egg yolks

FOR THE MERINGUE
4 organic egg whites
a pinch of salt
150 g (5 oz/1 cup) icing (powdered) sugar, sifted

HEAT THE OVEN to 160 C (325 F) Gas 3 (electric fan-assisted ovens should be set at 150 C). Butter a 24 cm (9 ½ inch) springform cake tin and line the base with baking parchment.

Make the cake. Sift the flour, baking powder and salt. Beat the butter, sugar and orange zest together until white and fluffy. Beat in the egg yolks one by one. Add about one-third of the flour mixture to the beaten butter-sugar-eggs mixture and fold in. Add one-third of the orange juice and fold in. Alternately add the remaining flour mixture and orange until evenly combined. Spread the cake mixture in the prepared cake tin. Set aside while you make the meringue.

Put the egg whites in a large, clean, grease-free bowl with a pinch of salt and whisk until they hold soft, slightly drooping peaks. Start whisking in the icing sugar, a tablespoon at a time, whisking well after each addition, and continue whisking until the egg whites are stiff and glossy. Spoon the meringue in an even layer over the cake mixture.

Place on a rack in the lower half of the oven (this is because the cake rises up quite alarmingly during baking). Bake until the sides of the cake have pulled away from the tin and the meringue topping is crisp and golden, 40 to 50 minutes.

Transfer to a wire rack and leave to cool completely in its tin. Run a knife around the sides of the cake to loosen before unmoulding. Use a palate knife or spatula to ease the cake off the tin base on to a serving dish. Serve with a spoonful of creamy yoghurt and a dusting of icing sugar.

CHOCOLATE CHESTNUT TORTE

Pure, utter, undiluted chocolate heaven - and it's not often that we can write that about a recipe. The glaze is optional; Victoria feels that it's quite decadent enough without it.

SERVES 10

FOR THE TORTE
500 g (1 lb) dark (bittersweet) chocolate
450 g (l lb) tin of unsweetened chestnut purée
125 ml (4 fl oz/½ cup) Cognac
6 tbsp double (heavy) cream
150 g (5 oz/⅔ cup) caster (granulated) sugar
125 g (4 oz/1 stick) softened butter
2 organic egg yolks
5 organic eggs
2 tbsp cornflour (cornstarch)

FOR THE GLAZE
125 ml (4 fl oz/½ cup) double (heavy) cream
125 g (4 oz) dark (bittersweet) chocolate, broken in to pieces

HEAT THE OVEN to 150 C (300 F) Gas 2 (electric fan-assisted ovens should be set to 140 C). Butter and flour a 24 cm (9 ½ inch) springform cake tin and line the base with baking parchment.

Melt the chocolate either in a microwave or in a bowl over a pan of barely simmering water and stir until smooth. Leave to cool until lukewarm.

Put the chestnut purée, Cognac and cream in a large bowl and, either with a food mixer or a wooden spoon, beat until smooth and creamy. Then beat in first the butter, then sugar, then the cooled, melted chocolate. Now beat in the beaten yolks and eggs in six batches, beating well after each addition, until the cake mixture is completely smooth. Lastly, sift over the cornflour and fold in.

Pour the cake mixture into the buttered, lined tin and bake until a skewer inserted into the centre of the cake comes out just slightly sticky, about 45 minutes. Cool completely on a wire rack before unmoulding – this will take at least 2 hours.

To make the glaze, heat the cream in a small pan over a low heat until just below simmering, then remove at once from the heat. Add the chocolate and leave to melt for a minute or so, then stir until smooth and glossy. Leave to cool until slightly thickened, about 30 minutes.

When the cake has cooled completely, unmould and spread the glaze evenly over the top of the cake. This lavish chocolate torte is best cut in rather smaller wedges than usual (it is so rich!) and served with a cup of unsweetened espresso coffee.

THINK AHEAD
You can bake this cake a day ahead - in fact it's quite a good idea to do so, as the cake must cool completely before serving. Store wrapped or in an airtight container, at a cool room temperature rather than in the fridge.

GOAT CHEESE & FIG CAKE

Eric says there are two reasons this cake came into being. This autumn there was a regular glut of cheap, ripe figs on the Portobello Market - that's the fig part. Every week Ian, a French cheesemonger drives over from Normandy and sells the best French cheeses your heart could desire on Fridays and Saturdays in the part of the Portobello Market that runs between Blenheim Crescent and Elgin Crescent - that's the goat's cheese part. Despite the fact that it's a recent creation, so many customers asked for the recipe that we felt obliged to include it here.

And does the end of the all too brief fig season render this recipe redundant? Why of course not! Simply use plums instead and bake a **Goat Cheese & Plum Cake.** You'll need 4 large red plums, cut in half. Arrange them skin side down.

And the goat's cheese? There's no need to despair if you are not local to Portobello and Ian's wonderful stall. Eric (admittedly rather grudgingly) says you can use any non-French goat cheese as long as it is fresh and creamy.

SERVES 8

3 tbsp caster (granulated) sugar,
5 fresh ripe figs, stalks trimmed, cut in half crosswise
175 g (6 oz/1 ½ cups) plain (all-purpose) flour
1 tbsp baking powder
175 g (6 oz/1 ½ sticks) butter, softened
175 g (6 oz/¾ cup + 2 tbsp) caster (granulated) sugar
200 g (7 oz) soft creamy goats cheese
3 organic eggs, beaten
1 tbsp apricot jam

Heat the oven to 180 C (350 F) Gas 5 (electric fan-assisted ovens should be set to 160 C). Butter a 24 cm (9 ½ inch) springform cake tin and line the base with buttered baking parchment. Sprinkle the buttered parchment evenly with sugar and arrange the halved figs, cut side down, over the sugar.

Make the cake. Sift the flour and baking powder. Beat the butter, sugar and goat's cheese together until white and fluffy. Beat in the eggs in three batches.

Sift over the flour and baking powder and gently fold in. Spread the cake mixture evenly over the figs.

Bake until the sides of the cake have pulled away from the tin and a skewer inserted in the middle of the cake comes out clean, about 50 minutes. Transfer to a wire rack and leave to cool completely in its tin. Run a knife around the sides of the cake to loosen before turning out.

To decorate, push the jam through a sieve into a small pan, then melt over a low heat. Brush the top of the cake with jam - concentrating especially on glazing the figs to bring out their beautiful jewel-like quality. Cut into wedges and dust lavishly with icing sugar to serve.

LIME CHEESECAKE WITH ALMOND CRUST

We have Silvena Rowe to thank for this luscious citrus cheesecake. Silvena is one of the most flamboyant cooks we know - tall, blond, Bulgarian and passionate about puddings - in her own words "dinner without dessert is like sex without a climax!"

SERVES 8

FOR THE FILLING
175 g (6 oz/¾ cup) caster (granulated) sugar
1 kg (2 lb) cream cheese
4 organic eggs, beaten
2 tbsp lime juice (allow 1-2 limes)
grated zest of 1 lime, preferably organic (wash and scrub well
            if not organic)

FOR THE CRUST
200 g (7 oz/2 cups) ground almonds
4 tbsp melted butter
4 tbsp caster (granulated) sugar

FOR THE TOPPING
300 ml (10 fl oz/1 ¼ cups) sour cream
4 tbsp caster (granulated) sugar
4 tbsp lime juice (allow 2-3 limes)

HEAT THE OVEN to 160 C (325 F) Gas 3 (electric fan-assisted ovens should be set at 150 C). Mix together the almonds, butter and sugar and press evenly into the bottom of a 24 cm (9 ½ inch) springform cake tin. Bake the base for 15 minutes to crisp and then let cool on a wire rack while you make the filling.

Place a dish of hot water on the bottom rack of the oven - this will moisten the air and stop a skin forming on the cheesecake.

Make the filling. Put the sugar and cream cheese in a large mixing bowl and beat with a rubber spatula until well-mixed. Add the eggs one at a time and beat until smooth. Gently fold in the lime juice and zest until smoothly combined.

Pour the filling into the cake tin and bake until the filling is just set around the edges but with a centre that looks still moist and wobbles when the tin is tapped, 30 to 40 minutes.

For the topping, mix the sour cream, sugar and lime juice together. As soon as the cheesecake is just set, spread this topping gently but evenly over the cheesecake. Return to the oven and cook for another 5 minutes before turning the oven off and leaving the cheesecake inside with the door ajar (or propped open with a wooden spoon) for 1 hour. Transfer the cheesecake to a wire rack and leave to cool completely in the tin. Cover and chill for at least 2 hours, overnight if you prefer, before serving.

Cut into wedges to serve. It needs no further adornment.

THINK AHEAD
Cheesecakes keep well for a few days in the fridge. Cover with cling film to avoid any unwanted savoury flavours being absorbed from whatever else is in the fridge.

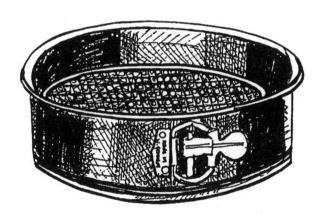

CHOCOLATE PEAR CAKE

The contrast between the dark chocolate sponge of the cake and the whiteness of the pears make this really rather a stunning dessert. Eric claims it came into being out of quite ignoble reasons, explaining that, as he gets older, he gets lazier, and he tries to keep cooking as simple as possible in the test kitchen, especially when it comes to baking. Consequently this must be the easiest chocolate cake mixture around.

SERVES 8

200 g (7 oz/1 ¼ sticks) butter
200 g (7 oz) dark (bittersweet) chocolate, broken into pieces
150 g (5 oz/⅔ cup) caster (granulated) sugar
3 organic eggs, beaten
1 tsp natural vanilla extract
100 g (3 ½ oz/¾ cup + 1 tbsp) plain (all-purpose) flour
1 tbsp baking powder
4 ripe fat pears, such as Comice (see ingredients note below)
4 tbsp caster (granulated) sugar

HEAT THE OVEN to 180 C (350 F) Gas 4 (electric fan-assisted ovens should be set at 160 C). Butter a 24 cm (9 ½ inch) springform cake tin and line the base with buttered baking parchment.

Put the butter in a small pan and gently melt over a low heat. When the butter has melted completely, remove from the heat and straightaway add the chocolate and sugar. Set aside for 15 minutes during which time the chocolate will melt, then stir until completely smooth. Transfer the melted chocolate mixture to a mixing bowl and leave to cool completely.

Add the eggs in three batches, beating until the mixture is smooth and glossy. Next, stir in the vanilla and sift over and gently but thoroughly fold in the flour and baking powder until evenly combined, with no white floury streaks showing. Set aside while you prepare the pears.

Peel and half the pears, cut out their stalk and flower ends and scoop out the core with a teaspoon (or melon baller, if you have one). Sprinkle the base of the tin evenly with the sugar. Arrange the pears cut side down over the sugar with their stalk ends pointing in towards the middle.

Spread the cake mixture evenly over the pears. Put into the oven and bake until the cake is well risen, the top is firm to the touch and slightly cracked but a skewer inserted into the middle of the cake comes out basically dry but with just a moist crumb or two still clinging to it, about 1 hour.

Transfer the cake to a wire rack and leave to cool in its tin before running a knife around the edge of the tin and turning the cake out. Serve warm or at room temperature, with thick creamy yoghurt or crème fraîche.

INGREDIENTS NOTE

If you haven't been able to plan ahead and buy your pears several days in advance to allow them to ripen, you can either resort to tinned pears or you'll need to poach your hard-as-a rock (they so often are, aren't they?) fresh pears until tender. Prepare the pears as directed, then place in a pan with a cupful of white sugar and 4 cupfuls of water, bring to the boil and simmer gently until just soft, 15 to 20 minutes. Does that sound like too much effort? Well, just use tinned!

BLACKBERRY APPLE RIPPLE CAKE

We like this glorious family-style cake with a spoonful of clotted cream for afternoon tea, but we love it served while still warm, with a scoop (or two) of vanilla ice cream, as a proper Sunday lunch pud. And don't panic if fresh blackberries are not available, frozen or tinned berries work very well indeed.

SERVES 8

FOR THE CAKE
250 g (8 oz/2 cups) plain (all-purpose) flour
1 tbsp baking powder
250 g (8 oz/2 sticks) butter, softened
250 g (8 oz/1 cup) caster (granulated) sugar
grated zest of 1 organic lemon (wash and scrub well if not organic)
4 organic eggs, beaten
1 tbsp lemon juice

FOR THE RIPPLE
2 eating apples, sliced
1 tbsp caster (granulated) sugar
$\frac{1}{2}$ tsp cinnamon
250 g (8 oz) blackberries

HEAT THE OVEN to 180 C (350 F) Gas 5 (electric fan-assisted ovens should be set to 160 C). Butter a 24 cm (9 $\frac{1}{2}$ inch) springform cake tin and line the base with baking parchment.

Make the cake. Sift the flour, baking powder and salt. Beat the butter, sugar and lemon zest together until white and fluffy. Beat in the eggs a little at a time, sprinkling in 1 tbsp of the flour when you have added about half the beaten eggs (this is to stop curdling). Add half the flour to the beaten butter-sugar-eggs mixture and fold in. Fold in the lemon juice, then fold in the remaining flour until evenly combined. Spread about two thirds of the cake mixture evenly over the base of the buttered and lined cake tin.

Sprinkle the apples with sugar and cinnamon and toss to coat well. Spread evenly over the cake mixture, then sprinkle the blackberries on top. Drop the remaining cake mixture in spoonfuls on top - there's no need to cover up the fruit completely, as the cake looks prettiest if bits of berry peep through.

114

Bake until the sides of the cake have shrunk slightly away from the tin, a skewer inserted into the cake comes and out clean and the top is golden and quite firm when you touch it, about 1 hour. Place on a wire rack and let cool in its tin for 15 minutes before unmoulding, when you can serve it hot like a pudding, or leave to cool completely, and then serve cold as a tea-time treat. Either way, thick cream is a must.

BLACKCURRANT & APPLE RIPPLE CAKE Replace the blackberries with 250 g (8 oz) blackcurrants.

BLUEBERRY & PEAR RIPPLE CAKE Replace the blackberries with 250 g (8 oz) blueberries and the apples with 2 ripe pears.

RASPBERRY & PEACH RIPPLE CAKE Replace the blackberries with 250 g (8 oz) raspberries, the apples with 2 ripe peaches and the cinnamon with 1 tsp natural vanilla extract.

REDCURRANT & APRICOT RIPPLE CAKE Replace the blackberries with 250 g (8 oz) redcurrants, the apples with 4 ripe apricots and the cinnamon with 1 tsp natural vanilla extract.

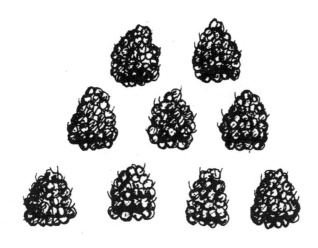

ROAST LEMON CAKE

Truly a lemon lovers' cake - a moist almond sponge studded with citrus-sharp, oven-candied lemon.

SERVES 8

FOR THE ROAST LEMONS
2 large lemons
3 tbsp caster (granulated) sugar

FOR THE CAKE
100 g (3 ½ oz/¾ cup + 1 tbsp) plain (all-purpose) flour
1 tbsp baking powder
75 g (2 ½ oz/¾ cup) ground (powdered) almonds
175 g (6 oz/1 ½ sticks) butter, softened
175 g (6 oz/¾ cup + 2 tbsp) caster (granulated) sugar
3 organic eggs, beaten
1 tbsp apricot jam

HEAT THE OVEN to 190 C (375 F) Gas 5 (electric fan-assisted ovens should be set at 180 C). Butter a 24 cm (9 ½ inch) springform cake tin and line the base with baking parchment.

Cut the lemons into quarters, then into eighths, and then slice each lemon eighth into pieces 1 cm (½ inch thick). Spread the lemon slices in an even layer in a small roasting pan and roast until softened and lightly caramelized around the edges, about 10 minutes. Sprinkle evenly with sugar and set aside to cool. Turn the oven down to 180 C (350 F) Gas 4 (electric fan-assisted ovens should be set at 160 C).

Make the cake. Sift the flour and baking powder and add the almonds. Beat the butter and sugar together until white and fluffy. Beat in the eggs a little at a time, sprinkling in 1 tbsp of the flour mixture when you have added about half the beaten eggs (this is to stop curdling). Gently fold in the flour mixture. Add the roast lemon pieces with any juices and fold in gently to distribute evenly. Spread the mixture evenly over the base of the prepared cake tin.

Bake until the sides of the cake have pulled away from the tin and a skewer inserted in the middle of the cake comes out clean, about 50 minutes. Transfer to a wire rack and leave to cool for 15 minutes. Run a knife around the sides of the cake to loosen before turning out.

To decorate, push the jam through a sieve into a small pan, then melt over a low heat. Brush the top and sides of the cake with jam. Decorate with red berries (when in season) or lemon segments.

CREAM CHEESE BROWNIES

We at Books for Cooks owe our brownie obsession to Debs Sonin, baker extraordinaire and former Books for Cooks Test Kitchen cook. While waiting for Debs to write her own definitive brownie cookbook, we satisfy our brownie urge with regular recipe testing of this all-American favourite. So we were thrilled when we came across this recipe of Nigella Lawson's (from her absolutely fabulous *How to be a Domestic Goddess*) - indeed these cream cheese brownies were immediately voted "Chocolate Confection of the Year" by all Books for Cooks staff. So we urge you to get out your cookie pan and make, bake and eat - you'll soon see why this recipe deserves a place in the brownie canon (*pace*, Debs).

MAKES 12 BROWNIES

200 g (7 oz/1 ½ sticks + 2 tbsp) butter, cut into cubes
200 g (7 oz) dark chocolate, broken into pieces
250 g (8 oz/1 cup + 2 tbsp) caster (granulated) sugar
3 organic eggs, beaten
1 tsp natural vanilla extract
125 g (4 oz/1 cup) plain (all-purpose) flour
½ tsp salt
300 g (10 oz/1 ¼ cups) cold cream cheese, thinly sliced (keep
    in the fridge until ready to use as it's easier to handle when chilled)

HEAT THE OVEN to 180 C (350 F) Gas 4. Position a rack in the centre of the oven. Line a 33 x 23 cm (13 x 9 inch) baking tin (pan) with baking parchment, letting it come up above the sides of the tray by about 5 cm (2 inches).

Melt the butter and the chocolate together in a heavy-based saucepan over very low heat, stirring constantly until smooth and glossy. Remove from the heat as soon as the chocolate has melted. Add the sugar, stir to dissolve, then leave to cool until tepid. Add the beaten eggs, a few tablespoons at a time, beating after each addition. The mixture will be very glossy. Add the vanilla. Gently fold in the flour and salt until just combined. Don't over mix.

Spread half the mixture evenly over the base of the prepared tin. Top with an even layer of the cream cheese slices, then pour over the rest of the brownie mixture. You may need to use a rubber spatula to distribute the mixture evenly over the cheese. Bake until the top is dry and the centre almost firm when lightly pressed but a toothpick inserted in the middle comes out still moist and fudgy, about 20 minutes. Don't overbake - that's the fatal error most people make. Place the tin on a wire rack and leave the brownie to cool completely in the tin before cutting up.

Use the overhanging paper to lift the brownie out of the tin, then cut into bars and carefully peel off the paper.

THINK AHEAD
You can certainly make these brownies a day ahead. Store in an airtight container at room temperature.

APRICOTS WITH LEMON & PISTACHIO MASCARPONE

A simply beautiful dessert from Nada Saleh's *Seductive Flavours of the Levant*. Arranged in concentric circles on a platter, these lovely sweet treats look almost jewel-like, the translucent orange of the apricots set into relief by the creamy white of the perfumed mascarpone and the fresh green of the ground pistachio.

You'll have some delicious apricot syrup left over. Nada suggests using it as a base for fruit salads; we like to dilute it with chilled sparkling mineral water when it makes the most refreshingly fruity cordial.

MAKES 20 TO 30 (depending on apricot size)

200 g (7 oz/1 cup) caster (granulated) sugar
300 ml (10 fl oz/1 ¼ cups) water
200 g (7 oz/1 ½ cups) dried apricots,
        soaked in cold water overnight
1 tbsp lemon juice
2 tbsp raw shelled pistachios (check that they're unsalted)
5 tbsp mascarpone

PLACE THE SUGAR and water in a medium pan and stir to dissolve. Bring to the boil over a medium heat and simmer for a minute before adding the drained apricots. Bring back to the boil, then adjust the heat and simmer steadily until the apricots have swollen and softened, about 15 minutes. Turn up the heat, add the lemon and simmer for another minute. Remove from the heat, scoop out the apricots with a slotted spoon and leave until the apricots and syrup are cool.

Put the pistachios in a food processor and pulse until finely ground, but not a complete powder. Spread the ground pistachios on a plate.

In a bowl, combine the mascarpone with 2 tbsp of the lemon-apricot syrup. Carefully open up the apricots with a small serrated knife. Fill each apricot with a little mascarpone. Now carefully dip the exposed mascarpone of each stuffed apricot in the ground pistachio. Place the apricots in a single layer on a tray and put into the fridge for about an hour to allow the mascarpone to firm up. Arrange the mascarpone-filled apricots prettily on a platter and serve chilled, with fresh mint tea.

THINK AHEAD
These delicious sweet treats can be made a day or two ahead of time. After the initial chilling the mascarpone will be firm and you can store them in an airtight container in layers.

BAKED PEAR & ALMOND CAKE

A rather architectural cake that never fails to create an impression on the test kitchen counter - even on Saturdays when the counter is loaded with seven or eight different sweet confections, all vying for attention. It's more pear than cake really - whole pears (stalk and skin and all) are baked in a buttery almond sponge. This rich and moist cake also makes a gorgeous pudding: serve with a large scoop of vanilla ice-cream and a generous swirl of melted chocolate.

Naturally, ripe pears are essential, and yet you must admit that sourcing ripe pears poses problems - indeed buying any ripe fruit from a supermarket is rather a challenge. So Eric recommends buying your pears a day or two ahead and letting them ripen before using.

SERVES 6

FOR THE CAKE
100 g (3 ½ oz/¾ cup + 1 tbsp) plain (all-purpose) flour
1 tbsp baking powder
75 g (2 ½ oz/¾ cup) ground (powdered) almonds
175 g (6 oz/1 ½ sticks) butter, softened
175 g (6 oz/¾ cup + 2 tbsp) caster (granulated) sugar
1 tsp natural vanilla extract
3 organic eggs, beaten
6 ripe slim pears (such as Conference)

FOR THE CHOCOLATE SAUCE
75 ml (2 ½ fl oz/5 tbsp) double (heavy) cream
75 g (2 ½ oz) dark (bittersweet) chocolate, broken into pieces

HEAT THE OVEN to 180 C (350 F) Gas 4 (electric fan-assisted ovens should be set at 160 C). Butter a 24 cm (9 ½ inch) springform cake tin and line the base with baking parchment.

Make the cake. Sift the flour and baking powder and add the almonds. Beat the butter, sugar and vanilla together until white and fluffy. Beat in the eggs a little at a time, sprinkling in a tablespoon of the flour mixture when you have added about half the beaten eggs (this is to stop curdling). Fold in the flour mixture gently but thoroughly. Spread the mixture evenly over the base of the prepared cake tin.

Cut a slice from the bottom of each pear to make a flat base - this is to make sure that your pears don't fall over during baking. Arrange six of the pears in a ring around the cake, stalk end up; leave a border of about 2 cm (¾ inch) cake mixture between the pear and the tin. Bake until the pears are tender, the sides of the cake have pulled away from the tin and a skewer inserted in the middle of the cake comes out clean, about 1 hour.

Transfer to a wire rack and leave to cool for 15 minutes. Run a knife around the sides of the cake to loosen before unmoulding. Use a palate knife or spatula to ease the cake off the tin base on to a serving dish.

For the chocolate sauce, heat the cream in a small pan until just below simmering point and remove at once from the heat. Add the chocolate and leave to melt for a minute or so, then stir until smooth and glossy.

Serve cut into wedges - each person should have a pear per slice - with a spoonful of fromage frais (good) or a scoopful of best vanilla ice cream (better), a generous swirl of chocolate and a lavish dusting of icing sugar.

CHOCOLATE TORTA DI NONNA

Yes, we know, *torta di nonna* is usually made with ricotta, but this version of Olivia's, with its easy-to-make but oh-so-delicious chocolate custard is much better, believe you us. Eventually we found we just couldn't wait for Olivia's visits to Books for Cooks to enjoy this gorgeous dessert, so Nessie begged the recipe and distributed it around all the girls in the shop.

FOR THE PASTRY   SERVES 8
100 g (3 ½ oz/7 tbsp) butter
300 g (10 oz/2 ¼ cups) plain (all-purpose) flour
1 tsp baking powder
a pinch of salt
100 g (3 ½ oz/½ cup) sugar
1 organic egg

FOR THE CREAM
150 g (5 oz/¾ cup) caster (granulated) sugar
2 organic eggs
3 tbsp plain (all-purpose) flour
500 ml (16 fl oz/2 cups) milk
200 (7 oz) dark (bittersweet) chocolate, broken into pieces
1 tsp natural vanilla extract
2 tbsp pine nuts

HEAT THE OVEN to 180 C (350 F) Gas 4 and put a baking sheet into the oven to preheat. Butter a 24 cm (9 ½ inch) springform cake tin and line the base with baking parchment.

Place the butter, flour, baking powder, salt and sugar in a food processor and pulse till the mixture resembles fine breadcrumbs. Add the egg and process until the dough comes together in moist crumbly bits - it shouldn't gather into a ball. If you don't have a food processor, do the whole thing as lightly as possible, using your fingertips to rub the butter into the flour and, when you add the egg, pinching the whole thing together into a crumbly dough.

Press and pat the pastry with your fingertips evenly over the base and up the sides of the tin to a thickness of about ½ cm (¼ inch). Don't fret if the pastry doesn't look perfectly and evenly smooth, it's a rustic Italian grandmother's pastry after all. Put the pastry-lined tin into the fridge to rest and chill (this helps reduce shrinking when the pastry is baked) for half an hour.

Make the filling. In a bowl, whisk the sugar and the eggs until thick, then whisk in the flour. Bring the milk just to the boil in a medium heavy-based saucepan over a low heat. Pour the hot milk into the egg mixture, whisking to blend. Return this custard mixture to the pan and bring to the boil, whisking all the time, until thickened. Remove from the heat. Add the chocolate pieces to the hot custard and stir until the chocolate has completely melted and is evenly combined (no streaks please) with the custard filling. Stir in the vanilla. Now pour this hot chocolate custard into the pastry case, sprinkle evenly with pine nuts and bake until just set, about 50 minutes. Place the tin on a wire rack and leave the torta to cool completely in its tin. Cut into wedges to serve.

VANILLA TORTA DI NONNA Make the filling as above but leave out the chocolate. Pour the hot custard into the pastry case, sprinkle with pine nuts and bake as directed.

FRUIT TORTA DI NONNA Omit the pine nuts. Peaches, nectarines, plums or apricots are the best fruit to choose. Have ready either 3 peaches or nectarines cut into 6 pieces, 4 large red plums quartered, or 500 g (1 lb) apricots or small plums, halved. Pour the hot custard into the pastry case and arrange the fruit skin side down over the custard. Bake as directed and dust lavishly with icing sugar when cool.

125

BOOKS FOR COOKS FRESH FIG MUFFINS

Pam and Eric have been on a bit of a muffin mission this year, putting all manner of muffin recipes to the test and baking a fresh batch of muffins every morning. For authentically sized Books for Cooks muffins you will need jumbo muffin pans and we highly recommend the silicon muffin pans from Lakeland Plastics (call 01539 488100). If your muffin pans are medium rather than larger, this batter will make about 12 standard muffins so you'll need 12 rather than 8 figs; bake for 12-15 minutes.

There was a glut of really ripe figs on Portobello Market this autumn and the prettiest use Eric found for his bargain trays of purple figs was setting a whole fig, opened out like a flower, on top of a lemon-scented muffin.

MAKES 8 LARGE MUFFINS

300 g (10 oz/2 $\frac{1}{4}$ cups) plain (all-purpose) flour
1 tbsp baking powder
$\frac{1}{4}$ tsp salt
175 g (6 oz/1 cup) fine cornmeal
150 g (5 oz/$\frac{3}{4}$ cup) caster (granulated) sugar
4 organic eggs, beaten
350 ml (12 fl oz/1 $\frac{1}{2}$ cups) milk
175 ml (6 fl oz/$\frac{3}{4}$ cup) sunflower oil
$\frac{1}{2}$ tsp natural vanilla extract
grated zest of 1 organic lemon (wash and scrub well if not organic)
1 tbsp lemon juice
8 fresh ripe figs, stalks trimmed
1 tbsp apricot jam, melted

HEAT THE OVEN TO 190 C (375 F) Gas 5 (electric fan-assisted ovens should be set to 180 C).

Sift the flour, baking powder and salt into a large mixing bowl. Stir in the cornmeal and the sugar and mix well to evenly blend, then make a well in the centre. It's important to mix these dry ingredients together well now, as you should keep mixing to a minimum when you add the wet ingredients.

In another bowl, beat the eggs, milk, oil, vanilla and lemon zest and juice together thoroughly, then pour into the well. Use a rubber spatula to fold the dry ingredients quikly and lightly into the wet ingredients. It doesn't matter if the batter is not evenly combined or even looks a bit lumpy. Completely smooth muffin batters mean over mixed muffin batters, which means tough, rubbery muffins.

Divide the mixture among the muffin cups, filling up about three-quarters full. With a small serrated knife, cut each fig almost but not quite into quarters. Open up each fig like a flower and place one cut fig on the top of each muffin. Bake until the edges shrink from the sides of the cups and a toothpick inserted into the muffins comes out clean, 20 to 25 minutes. Let cool for 5 minutes before turning out onto a wire rack to cool. Glaze the figs by brushing each one with melted apricot jam. Eat your muffins warm or at room temperature. Eric likes to elevate his muffins into a really rather indulgent pud by serving them with creamy yoghurt and a drizzle of melted chocolate.

BOOKS FOR COOKS BANANA MUFFINS Eric likes to fill his banana muffins with a big chunk of banana rather than the more usual diced banana. Sift 1 tsp ground cinnamon with the flour mixture. Omit the lemon zest and juice. Replace the figs with 2 ripe bananas. Spoon the batter into the muffin cups. Cut each banana crosswise into 4 equally sized pieces. Push a banana piece into each cup of muffin batter, taking care not to totally submerge it in batter - it's prettiest when you can see the banana peeping through the muffin crust. Bake as directed.

BOOKS FOR COOKS BERRY MUFFINS Omit lemon and figs and replace with 125 g (4 oz/1 cup) blueberries, blackberries, black or redcurrants or raspberries. Stir the berries gently and quickly into the batter before spooning into the muffin cups. You can also use strawberry halves, but it's best to add them directly to the muffin batter when the batter is in the muffin cups. Push the strawberries down into the batter with your fingers - this way the strawberries don't just sink to the bottom of the muffin.

THINK AHEAD
You can bake the muffins up to 2 days ahead. Store in an airtight container at room temperature and refresh in a 150 C (300 F) Gas 3 oven for 5-10 minutes before serving.

SARAH'S CHOCOLATE CHIP COOKIES

Every morning Sarah rustles up freshly baked cookies for our workshop customers to have with their coffee upstairs in the workshop kitchen. These soft and chewy choc chip cookies (based on the original Toll House cookie) are our absolute favourites. She says "This is a versatile cookie base that can be altered simply by changing the chocolate, adding nuts, raisins, spices, toffee nibs, M&M's or whatever your imagination desires!"

MAKES ABOUT 30 COOKIES

150 g (5 oz/1 cup + 2 tbsp) plain (all-purpose) flour
¾ tsp baking powder
a pinch of salt
125 g (4 oz/1 stick) butter, softened
125 g (4 oz/½ cup) soft brown sugar
50 g (1 ¾ oz/¼ cup) caster (granulated) sugar
1 tsp natural vanilla extract
1 organic egg, separated
175 g (6 oz) dark (bittersweet chocolate), coarsely chopped

Heat the oven to 180 C (350 F) Gas 4 (electric fan-assisted ovens should be set at 170 C). Line two baking sheets with baking parchment.

Sift the flour, baking powder and salt together. Using a hand-held mixer, beat the butter, brown and white sugars and vanilla until light and fluffy. Beat in the egg yolk, beating well to thoroughly combine. Sarah says that adding the yolk separately emulsifies the batter and prevents curdling. Beat in a tablespoon of the flour mixture, then beat in the egg white. Add the remaining flour mixture in three batches, blending just until the mixture forms a dough. Fold in the chopped chocolate. Drop tablespoons of the cookie dough on the baking parchment lined baking sheets, spacing about 5 cm (2 inches) apart.

It's best to cook one baking sheet of cookies at a time, but if you are pushed for time and want to bake them both together, be sure to rotate the baking sheets halfway through baking for even browning. Bake until the cookies are just slightly coloured on top and golden around the edges, 10 to 12 minutes. Sarah says the key to choc chip cookie perfection is to bake the cookies until just set - if you over bake them, they'll be crunchy rather than chewy in texture, although still quite delicious in flavour. Place the baking sheet on a wire rack and let the cookies cool slightly so that they firm up, about 3 minutes, then transfer the cookies from the baking sheet on to wire racks to cool completely.

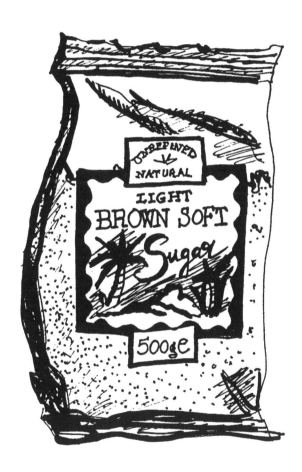

RED PLUM CARAMEL CAKE

Eric's upside down fruit caramel cake is a Books for Cooks perennial. On Saturdays you'll generally find the Test Kitchen counter laden with caramel cakes in a variety of fruit flavours, depending on what's on the Portobello market stalls.

You'll notice that Eric doesn't make the cake batter like a pound cake (creaming the butter and sugar first and beating in the eggs bit by bit etc) but uses a quick all-in-one method. The important thing here is to make sure the butter is nice and soft - what French call *beurre en pommade*, which means "butter the consistency of face cream" and this is rather an apt description. Kitchen French is the most precise culinary language in the world, you see. Anyway, make sure you take your butter out of the fridge in time or wack it in the microwave or oven for a quick soften.

SERVES 8

FOR THE CARAMEL
175 g (6 oz/¾ cup + 2 tbsp) caster (granulated) sugar
6 tbsp water
4 large red plums, halved

FOR THE CAKE
150 g (5 oz/ 1 ¼ cups) plain (all-purpose) flour
2 tsp baking powder
175 g (6 oz/1 ½ sticks) butter, softened
175 g (6 oz/¾ cup + 2 tbsp) caster (granulated) sugar
4 tbsp ground (powdered) almonds
4 organic eggs, beaten
1 tsp natural vanilla extract

HEAT THE OVEN to 150 C (300 F) Gas 2. Butter a 24 cm (9 ½ inch) springform cake tin and line the base with baking parchment.

Place the sugar and water in a heavy-based pan over a low heat. Stir constantly with a wooden spoon to dissolve the sugar. Don't let the liquid boil until the sugar has completely dissolved to form a clear syrup. Now raise the heat to medium and bring the syrup to the boil. Boil rapidly until the syrup starts to turn brown around the edge of the pan. Lower the heat and cook the sugar to a dark golden brown. You shouldn't stir sugar as it cooks, just swirl the pan once or twice so that it colours evenly. As soon as the caramel is ready, pour immediately into the buttered tin. Arrange the plums skin side up over the caramel.

Sift the flour and baking powder into a large bowl. Add butter, sugar, almonds, eggs and vanilla. Beat until smooth and evenly blended, 1-2 minutes. Spread the cake mixture over the fruit. Bake until the top is golden brown and the sides of the cake have pulled away from the tin, about 50 minutes.

Transfer to a wire rack and leave to cool for a few minutes, then run a knife around the sides of the cake and turn out onto a serving dish. If any pieces of fruit stick to the paper, don't despair, you can use a spatula to remove and press them back into place. You can serve the cake warm or at room temperature. We serve it with a dusting of icing sugar and a dollop of thick, creamy yoghurt.

APRICOT CARAMEL CAKE Replace the plums with apricots. As apricots vary wildly in size, it's best to buy 500 g (1 lb).

APPLE or PEAR CARAMEL CAKE Replace the plums with 3 apples or pears, quartered.

PEACH or NECTARINE CARAMEL CAKE Replace the plums with 3 peaches or nectarines, quartered.

STRAWBERRY CARAMEL CAKE This looks like a bit of a car crash, but is very delicious. Make it when you have a glut of strawberries or when the stallholders on Portobello are selling off strawberries cheap on Saturday afternoon. Replace the plums with 1 kg (2 1b) ripe strawberries; don't bother to arrange nicely, but simply spread in an even layer.

MANGO CARAMEL CAKE Replace the plums with 3 medium sliced mangoes or (more economical) 1 tin of drained sliced mangoes.

PINEAPPLE CARAMEL CAKE. Replace the plums with 8 pineapple rings or the drained contents of 1 medium (about 425 g/14½ oz) tin (250 g/8 oz drained weight).

Basics

SHORTCRUST & SWEET PASTRY

An easy, good-tempered pastry that will line a 24 cm (9 ½) tart tin. We urge removable bases because they do make life easier when it comes to unmoulding your finished savoury or sweet tart. In fact, a great tip is to rest the tart tin on an upturned mixing bowl, and the tart will practically unmould itself as the outer metal rim just slips off.

We recommend blind baking (pre-baking) the pastry case. You will need a baking sheet and some baking beans - dried beans or rice will do just as well as the purpose-built ceramic ones. There are few things more disappointing than soggy undercooked pastry when you have gone to all the trouble of preparing a superlative tart filling, so judge the cooking time by the colour rather than by the clock and bake your pastry case until a light biscuit brown.

SHORTCRUST PASTRY

175 g (6 oz/1 ½ cups) plain (all-purpose) flour sifted
a good pinch of salt
90 g (3 oz/¾ stick) very cold butter, cubed
1 organic egg yolk plus 1 tbsp cold water, or 4-5 tbsp water

LIGHTLY BUTTER A 24 cm (9 ½ inch) tart tin and put it into the refrigerator.

Put the flour and salt in a food processor and aerate with a couple of quick on/off pulses. Add the butter and process till the mixture resembles fine breadcrumbs. Add the yolk and water (if necessary) and process until the pastry just draws together. Turn it out on to a lightly floured work surface and knead briefly to form a flat round.

If you don't have a food processor, do the whole thing as lightly as possible, using your fingertips to rub the butter into the flour and, when you add the liquid, pinching the whole thing into a dough.

Unless it's a very hot day, you should roll the pastry out straightaway without chilling first. Roll out to a round at least 5 cm (2 inches) larger than the tin, wrap around the rolling pin, lift into place and unroll loosely over the chilled tin. Gently lift and press the pastry into the tin to line, then roll the rolling pin over the top of the tin to trim the excess pastry. Put the pastry lined tin into the refrigerator to rest for at least an hour, or into the freezer for 15 minutes, if you're pushed for time. Do not, under any circumstances, throw the leftover pastry away, but roll it into a ball, wrap in cling film and keep at room temperature until you take your baked pastry case out of the oven (see pastry problems below).

SWEET PASTRY

Use the quantities and method given above, but mix in 45 g (1 ½ oz/5 tbsp) sifted icing sugar with the flour and salt, and add ½ tsp natural vanilla extract with the egg yolk and, if necessary, water. We advise using icing sugar as its fine starchiness, as opposed to the graininess of ordinary sugar, contributes to the pastry's manageability.

BAKING BLIND (PRE-BAKING)

Put a baking sheet in the oven and heat to 190 C (375 F) Gas 5. Having a hot baking sheet in the oven helps the pastry case cook more evenly, otherwise the sides tend to cook before the base.

Line the chilled pastry case with baking parchment, fill with baking beans and cook for 10 minutes. Carefully remove the beans and paper and cook for another 10 minutes or a little longer, until a light biscuit brown.

INDIVIDUAL TARTLETS

To make six 12 cm (5 inch) shortcrust pastry cases, you will need 250 g (8 oz/2 cups) plain (all-purpose) flour, a good pinch of salt, 125 g (4 oz/1 stick) really cold butter, 2 organic egg yolks plus 2 tbsp cold water, or 7-8 tbsp cold water. Follow our instructions for making shortcrust pastry (see page 114).

To line your tins (we use fluted 12 cm (5 inch) fluted tart tins with removeable bases), arrange the tins close together on a baking sheet. Roll out the pastry until about 10 cm (4 inches) larger than all the tins bunched together. Wrap the pastry round the rolling pin and unroll gently and loosely over the tins, trying not to stretch it. Carefully lift and press the pastry into the tins, then roll the rolling pin over the tins to trim the pastry to a neat edge. Don't throw the trimmings away, but keep to patch the baked pastry in case it cracks during baking (see page 136). Put into the fridge or freezer to chill before blind baking (pre-baking) (see above).

PASTRY PROBLEMS

Having everything very cold really helps; you might like to put your butter cubes in the freezer for 5 minutes extra chilling to keep everything nice and cold, while some people keep their flour in the freezer both for pastry purposes and because it keeps better.

If your pastry is too crumbly, roll it out between two pieces of cling film (plastic wrap). If it is too soft because the ingredients are too warm, or you have added too much liquid, chill it first, until firm but not rock-hard, before rolling out in between cling film. Cling film, as you can see, is but a little short of a universal panacea, working wonders with all kinds of pastry problems.

Well, you lined the tin, rested the pastry and baked it blind. Hopefully you now have a perfect pastry case before you. If, however, you find you have a less than perfect pastry case with one or two or lots of little cracks in it (evil little cracks though which the tart filling threatens to seep), do not despair. This is where your leftover pastry will come to the rescue. Gently press scraps of the leftover raw pastry to the cracks in the hot pastry shell and the heat will stick the raw and the cooked pastry together and seal up the cracks. Easy as pie.

Menus

DINNER IN A DASH

Minted Pea Soup
(see page 25)

Chicken Cooked with Bay, Garlic & White Wine
(see page 62)
Lemon, Mustard & Parsley Mash
(see page 76)

Pineapple Caramel Cake
(see page 132)

NEW FOOD FOR FRIENDS

Ginger & Lime Marinated Tiger Prawns with Avocado Salsa
(see page 48)

Indonesian Marinated Chicken with Roast Sweet Potatoes & Peppers
(see page 30)

Lime Cheesecake with Almond Crust
(see page 110)

VEGETARIAN CELEBRATION MEAL

Grilled Courgette, Feta & Mint Salad
(see page 36)
Olive Bread with Onion Jam
(see page 84)

Crespelle with Ricotta, Spinach & Rosemary
(see page 43)

Baked Pear & Almond cake
(see page 122)
Chocolate Sauce & Best Vanilla Ice Cream

DO-AHEAD DINNER

Sweet Potato Soup with Ginger & Coconut
(see page 18)

Braised Duck with Soy, Ginger & Star Anise
(see page 46)
Chicory, Pear & Watercress Salad
(see page 92)

Books for Cooks Chocolate Cake
(see page 196)
Crème Fraîche

MIDSUMMER BUFFET LUNCH

Mediterranean Grilled Chicken Salad with Roast Garlic & Basil Dressing
(see page 58)
Ricotta & Tomato Tart
(see page 56)
Focaccia with Roast Red Onions
(see page 82)
Carrot Salad with Toasted Sesame Seeds
(see page 78)
Chilli Chickpea Yoghurt Salad
(see page 77)

Chocolate Fudge Brownies
(see page 100)
Summer Berries & Thick Cream

A LIGHT LUNCH FOR FRIENDS

Tomato, Lentil & Orange Soup
(see page 12)

Roast Pumpkin & Chickpea Salad with Sun-Dried Tomato Dressing
(see page 70)

Goat Cheese & Plum Cake
(see page 108)
Thick & Creamy Yoghurt

TABLE OF EQUIVALENTS

LIQUIDS CONVERSIONS

Metric	Imperial	US
30 ml	1 fl oz	2 tbsp
45 ml	1 ½ fl oz	3 tbsp
60 ml	2 fl oz	¼ cup
75 ml	2 ½ fl oz	⅓ cup
90 ml	3 fl oz	⅓ cup + 1 tbsp
100 ml	3 ½ fl oz	⅓ cup + 2 tbsp
125 ml	4 fl oz	½ cup
150 ml	5 fl oz	⅔ cup
175 ml	6 fl oz	¾ cup
200 ml	7 fl oz	¾ cup + 2 tbsp
250 ml	8 fl oz	1 cup
275 ml	9 fl oz	1 cup + 2 tbsp
300 ml	10 fl oz	1 ¼ cups
325 ml	11 fl oz	1 ⅓ cups
350 ml	12 fl oz	1 ½ cups
375 ml	13 fl oz	1 ⅔ cups
400 ml	14 fl oz	1 ¾ cups
450 ml	15 fl oz	1 ¾ cups +2 tbsp
500 ml	16 fl oz	1 pint (2 cups)
600 ml	1 pint	2 ½ cups
900 ml	1 ½ pint	3 ¾ cups
1 litre	1 ¾ pints	4 cups

USEFUL EQUIVALENTS

Flour
1 cup	4 oz

Cocoa
1 cup	3 oz

Flaked Almonds
1 cup	3 oz

Ground Almonds
1 cup	3 ¾ oz

Chopped Nuts
1 cup	4 oz

White Sugar
1 cup	7 oz

Brown Sugar
1 cup	8 oz

Icing Sugar
1 cup	4 oz

OVEN TEMPERATURES

Celsius	Fahrenheit	Gas
120	250	½
140	275	1
150	300	2
160	325	3
180	350	4
190	375	5
200	400	6
220	425	7
230	450	8
240	475	9
260	500	10

Note: Reduce the temperature by 20 C (68 F) for fan-assisted ovens

WEIGHT CONVERSIONS

Metric	UK/US
15 g	½ oz
30 g	1 oz
45 g	1 ½ oz
60 g	2 oz
75 g	2 ½ oz
90 g	3 oz
100 g	3 ½ oz
125 g	4 oz
150 g	5 oz
175 g	6 oz
200 g	7 oz
250 g	8 oz
275 g	9 oz
300 g	10 oz
325 g	11 oz
350 g	12 oz
375 g	13 oz
400 g	14 oz
450 g	15 oz
500 g	1 lb

PLEASE NOTE: A few golden rules of measuring: always stick religiously to one system, never mix and match. When measuring liquids, place the jug on a flat surface, bend down and check for accuracy at eye level. When using cups, spoon the ingredient into the cup, mounding slightly, and level off with the back of a knife. Do not use the cup as a scoop or tap the cup on the work surface. Bear in mind that these tables are approximate; they do not completely conform to the official conversions, but we have found them useful.

FOOD FINDS IN NOTTING HILL

These are the shops local to Books for Cooks that we couldn't do without. If you are coming to visit us, we strongly advise a visit to at least one of them as well.

CORNEY & BARROW
194 Kensington Park Road, W11
020 7221 5122
Mon-Sat 10.30-9pm
All the wines that accompany our workshop tastings are specially selected and supplied by this excellent wine merchant, which also stocks estate-bottled olive oils.

FRESH & WILD
210 Westbourne Grove, W10
020 7229 1063
Mon-Fri 8am-9pm
Sat 8am-8pm Sun 10am-7pm
Excellent (and our most local) organic supermarket(with juice bar) formerly known as Wild Oats.

R. GARCIA & SONS
248 Portobello Road, W11
020 7221 6119
Tues-Sat 9.30am-6-30pm Sun11am-6pm
This Spanish delicatessen has been in the Garcia family for three generations now. It is our favourite shop of them all.

LE MAROC
94 Goldbourne Road, W10
020 8968 9783
Mon-Sat 9am-7pm
Spicy merguez, preserved lemons and fabulous flatbreads as well as glazed earthenware tagine pots are available at this Moroccan delicatessen.

MR. CHRISTIAN'S
11 Elgin Crescent, W11
020 7229 0501
Mon-Thurs 7am-7pm Fri 6am-7pm
Sat 5.30am-6.30pm Sun 7am-5pm
This deli, established over 20 years ago, is a Notting Hill institution, famous for its fabulous bread stall outside the store on Saturdays.

PORTOBELLO MARKET
Portobello Road, W11
Mon-Wed 8am-6pm
Thu 9am-1pm Sat 7am-7pm
Friday is the best day and Brian keeps the stall to go for, in between Blenheim and Elgin Crescents.

THE SPICE SHOP
1 Blenheim Crescent, W11
020 7221 4448
Mon-Sat 9.30am-6pm Sun 11am-5pm
This tiny, nose-twitching shop across the road from Books for Cooks sells fresh herbs, nuts, dried grains and pulses as well as every spice and culinary flavouring the world has to offer!

TAWANA
18-20 Chepstow Road, W2
020 7221 6316
Mon-Sun 9.30am-8pm
Although specializing in Thai ingredients ingredients (including fresh herbs, fruit and vegetables), you'll also find a broad selection of items from all over South-East Asia.

THE TEA AND COFFEE PLANT
170 Portobello Road, W11
020 7221 8137
Mon-Sat 8am-6.30pm Sun 10am-5pm
We buy our special blend of coffee beans as well as our teas (all organic) from this functional store where they roast and grind right in front of you! They also sell the fairtrade organic chocolate that we use in all our chocolate baking.

RECIPE LIST

SOUPS

MAIN COURSES

SALADS & SIDES

SWEET THINGS